The Choral Music of Twentieth-Century Women Composers

Elisabeth Lutyens, Elizabeth Maconchy, and Thea Musgrave

Catherine Roma

The Scarecrow Press, Inc.
Lanham, Maryland • Toronto • Oxford
2006

SCARECROW PRESS, INC.

Published in the United States of America
by Scarecrow Press, Inc.
A wholly owned subsidiary of
The Rowman & Littlefield Publishing Group, Inc.
4501 Forbes Boulevard, Suite 200, Lanham, Maryland 20706
www.scarecrowpress.com

PO Box 317
Oxford
OX2 9RU, UK

British Library Cataloguing in Publication Information Available

Library of Congress Cataloging-in-Publication Data
Roma, Catherine.
  The choral music of twentieth-century women composers : Elisabeth Lutyens,
Elizabeth Maconchy, and Thea Musgrave / Catherine Roma.
  p. cm.
  Includes bibliographical references (p.   ) and index.
  ISBN 0-8108-5029-X (pbk. : alk. paper)
  1. Choral music--Great Britain--20th century. 2. Lutyens, Elisabeth, 1906-
Choral music. 3. Maconchy, Elizabeth, 1907- Choral music. 4. Musgrave,
Thea. Choral music. 5. Music by women composers--Great Britain--20th
century--History and criticism. I. Title.
  ML1506.R66 2005
  782.5'092'241--dc22   2005018758

⊖™ The paper used in this publication meets the minimum requirements of
American National Standard for Information Sciences—Permanence of
Paper for Printed Library Materials, ANSI/NISO Z39.48-1992.
Manufactured in the United States of America.

For years of patience and unconditional love
Dorothy Eleanor Smith

For continued mentoring and support
Karin Pendle

and

In loving memory of my parents,
Elisa Felici and Emilio Roma

Contents

Contents

Figures

Musical Examples

Foreword

Women's voices—where can they be found? How can they be defined? How have they been muted, silenced, adapted to the dominant male culture of their times and places? These are questions being asked of the artistic products of women that have been recovered, rediscovered, and reread since the resurgence of feminism in recent years drew to our attention the messages and lessons that needed to be reclaimed as part of our heritage. It seems ironic, then, that the field of music scholarship, dealing with an art in which the voice is often literally present, has been slow to take up the challenge of finding and defining the contributions and roles of women. Yet it can no longer be denied that women at all times and in all places have both created and performed music. Their voices need to be heard if we are to comprehend the scope and variety of the musical experience throughout history.

For some time, twentieth-century Britain seemed an ideal place for the development of women's musical talents. Women performers, such as soprano Jane Manning, commissioned and presented works by women; women impresarios, such as Anne Macnaghten and Iris Lemare, developed concert series that promoted new music by composers of both sexes equally; major institutions—the BBC or various choral or chamber groups, for example—commissioned women to write for them; and the Society of Women Musicians stood as a proud and necessary support group. In the background, people like Ralph Vaughan Williams and Gustav Holst, key figures in the English musical renaissance of the twentieth century, led British audiences and institutions to a new appreciation of their own musical heritage. Although, as Nicola LeFanu demonstrated in her study, "Master Musician: An Impregnable Taboo?" (*Contact* 31, 1987), these favorable conditions for women were not to continue unchallenged, they nonetheless provided a foundation for the rise to prominence of many first-rate female talents, among them LeFanu's own mother, Elizabeth Maconchy. And it is here, in the middle decades of the twentieth century, that we find a chorus of women's voices that deserve to be heard.

Despite a subsequent decline in the number of women writing music and having it performed by major soloists and ensembles, the voices of British women nonetheless sounded forth. They were heard most prominently in the works of Scotch-born Thea Musgrave, still a formidable figure in the world of modern music. Nor has the younger generation been idle: within the past decade or two the world has heard the voices of such admirable figures as Judith Weir, Rhian Samuel, and Nicola LeFanu herself—women whose music, live and on record, has reached an international audience.

Where better to begin the search for women's voices than in choral music, a genre in which individual uniqueness takes on a collective expression, conveyed to an audience not just through musical content but through content presented by means of the physical voices of those who perform it? Catherine Roma, a conductor and scholar of wide experience and growing national reputation, brings to this study of choral writing by British women an infectious enthusiasm and a genuine appreciation of this music. Whether describing the struggles of Elisabeth Lutyens to find her own voice, relating how Elizabeth Maconchy reveals her own distinctive voices even in her earliest works, or quoting Thea Musgrave's wish that "I hope I have a style that is recognizable and individual," Roma provides material of value both to the student and to the conductor. The amount and variety of choral music by these women, their contemporaries, and their successors that emerges from these pages constitutes a repertoire worthy of notice, performance, and recording. For only as we get acquainted with this and other music by women can we begin to apprehend the uniqueness and validity of what women composers have to communicate.

Karin Pendle
Professor Emerita, Musicology
College-Conservatory of Music
University of Cincinnati

Preface

This book brings to the attention of choral conductors, and those interested in contemporary music and music by women, the exciting, accessible choral works of three contemporary British composers. Although relatively unknown in the United States, Elisabeth Lutyens (1906-1983), Elizabeth Maconchy (1907-1994), and Thea Musgrave (1928-) earned solid reputations in the Britain of their times. Although all three have written music in various genres, choral music has constituted an important part of their output. Their music reveals them to be substantial, prolific, collegial composers who are representative of major trends in twentieth-century British choral composition.

The compositional techniques used by Lutyens, Maconchy, and Musgrave vary. Elisabeth Lutyens is often described as a musical pioneer because of her use of twelve-tone technique. Set theory is the basis of the analytical approach used in the Lutyens chapter, which also notes that her departures from the strict practice of serial writing are always highly personal and imaginative.

Maconchy described her own techniques as "an impassioned argument," and compositional techniques found in her thirteen string quartets—such as contrapuntal textures and short, generative cells, used skillfully and economically—are discernible in her choral works. Maconchy's harmonic language is tonal, and she incorporates a high degree of chromatic color.

Thea Musgrave's music encompasses many modes of expression. Her earliest choral works feature tonal diatonic writing. Although her style shows a gradual movement toward serial techniques in works for other media, this approach is never developed in any choral setting. Out of her short-lived serial period evolves a free chromatic style in which there is no actual tonal function, but rather some degree of tonal expectation. Her personal idiomatic style is a combination of many musical techniques.

This work, a contribution to the growing literature on women in music, thus demonstrates the great diversity of approaches and techniques used by composers of the twentieth century.

Acknowledgments

The motto of the most important school I attended read: "BEHOLD, I SET BE-FORE THEE AN OPEN DOOR" (Germantown Friends School, Philadelphia). There have been a significant number of teachers since childhood who inspired me and gave me courage. Louise Christine Rebe, Dorothea Persichetti, and Mary Emma Brewer nourished in me not only a deep love of music but also a lifelong curiosity. Other important teachers and powerful influences have been Robert Fountain, Helmuth Rilling, and especially Elaine Brown.

Conversations with Allen Sapp about the compositional climate in Britain in the 1960s and the inspired craft of Lutyens, Maconchy, and Musgrave were en-lightening. Karin Pendle continues to encourage and guide me and is a mentor in the truest sense of the word. It is this ongoing relationship that deepens the value of my days spent at the College-Conservatory of Music.

Glyn Perrin, the musical executor to the late Lutyens; Roger Wright at the British Music Information Center; Sheila MacCrindle at Chester Music; and the hospitality of Paul and Marcia Thompson made my first solo trip to London for research extraordinary. Thanks to Jean Leavitt Finch, Deborah Meem, David Smith, and Douglas McConnell, friends and great teachers who assisted in areas of their expertise. Josh Mitteldorf's contribution is inestimable. Marilyn Ebertz, Winnie Goodridge, and Michael Petersen assisted in the final stages with editing and pertinent questions, and all share a miraculous eye for detail.

The final stage of preparation materialized with the chance meeting of Liann Curtis and the extraordinary surprise exchange with Mark Palkovic. With Mark's previous editorial experience and calm and steady sense of pacing, I was able to push through to completion.

Heartfelt thanks to the women of MUSE Cincinnati's Women's Choir and members of the St. John's Unitarian Universalist Church Choir who provided a supportive and loving community. And most of all for the enduring love that nurtured me throughout, I thank Dorothy Smith, formerly of Yellow Springs, Ohio, who supplied the quiet space in Tully House, with warmth, patience, encouragement, and love. Her incalculable support for this lengthy project continued at the Merry Maidens Hanfield House in Cincinnati, Ohio.

Appreciation and thanks are also given to the following people and publishers for permission to reprint the following materials:

Glyn Perrin, musical executor to the late Elisabeth Lutyens, for permission to reprint excerpts from Olivan Press: *Requiem for the Living* © 1948, *Counting Your Steps* © 1972.

Arnold Broido, director of performance promotion for Theodore Presser, for permission to reprint excerpts from Novello: "Song of the Burn" by Thea Musgrave © 1974, "John Cook" by Thea Musgrave © 1963, *Rorate Coeli* by Thea Musgrave © 1977, *The Last Twilight* by Thea Musgrave © 1981, "O caro m'è il sonno" by Thea Musgrave © 1978, "The Lord's Prayer" by Thea Musgrave © 1984, "Country of the Stars" by Elisabeth Lutyens © 1963, "Verses of Love" by Elisabeth Lutyens © 1971.

Alan Woolgar, copyright manager, for permission to reprint excerpts from Schott and Co. Ltd.: *Excerpta Tractati Logico-Philosophici* © 1965.

James Rushton, managing director of Chester Music London, for permission to reprint excerpts from Chester Music: *Nocturnal* by Elizabeth Maconchy © 1981, "Siren's Song" by Elizabeth Maconchy © 1974, excerpts from *Creatures* by Elizabeth Maconchy © 1979 ("The Snail," "Cat!"), *The Leaden Echo and the Golden Echo* by Elizabeth Maconchy © 1978, excerpts from *Four Madrigals* by Thea Musgrave © 1953 ("With serving still," "Tanglid I was," "At most mischief," "Hate whom ye list"), "Memento Creatoris" by Thea Musgrave © 1967.

Bruce Hunter of David Higham Associates for Lutyens' *All Our Tomorrows* and *Composer's Concourse.*

Sally-Ann Sweet, Permissions Department, Routledge and Kegal Paul, Ltd., for permission to reprint *Tractatus Logic-Philosophicus* by Ludwig Wittgenstein, translated by Pears and McGuinness.

Florence B. Eichen, permissions manager, Penguin USA, for "Men in New Mexico," from *The Complete Poems of D. H. Lawrence* by D. H. Lawrence, edited by V. de Sola Pinto & F. W. Roberts © 1964, 1971 by Angelo Ravagli and C. M. Weekly, executors of the estate of Frieda Lawrence Ravagli. Used by permission of Viking Penguin, a division of Penguin Books, USA Inc. Margaret Pepper of Laurence Pullinger, Ltd. and the Estate of Frieda Lawrence Ravagli for "Men in New Mexico" by D. H. Lawrence (U. K. and Commonwealth).

Introduction

Historical Perspective

Over the last forty years, musicologists have written about the English Musical Renaissance of the twentieth century, describing the burst of compositional activity in a variety of musical styles exhibited by the works of twentieth-century English composers. In 1946 Wilfrid Mellers observed:

> If one reflects on the situation in English music at the turn of the century it seems astonishing that the creative spark should have been rekindled at all; the scope and variety of creative musical activity in this country today is certainly greater than any impartial intelligent observer would have bargained for thirty or even twenty years ago.[1]

This musical renaissance, often ascribed to the abandoning of German compositional models and the rediscovery of England's own musical past, resulted largely from the work of Gustav Holst and Ralph Vaughan Williams. A glance back to 1919 will prove insightful:

> Musicians of today are gradually making the discovery that, after a prolonged period of relative sterility, England has become within a generation or two, one of the most copious contributors to contemporary music. This modern renaissance has coincided with the birth of a new social spirit, the effects of which have already proved far-reaching. We still find contemporary composers of merit using melodic outlines recalling those of the German *Lied*, whilst others, like Vaughan Williams, are fashioning phrases such as any Englishman knows by instinct to be of indigenous growth. Forerunners of the movement are now generally classed as academics, such as Stanford, Parry and Mackenzie. Then one

would proceed to its dawn which opens with Elgar and brings forward the names of William Wallace, Ethel Smyth, Granville Bantock—Delius represents the more cosmopolitan aspect of this section. Even today one can point to gifted composers who are still only in the convalescent stage. But the standard of revolt itself was raised in the citadel itself, that is to say, in the institution where the cult of Brahms was at its highest, and several of whose former pupils are now among the most independent of the outstanding figures of English music. At their head one would place Vaughan Williams, whose works contain in an exceptional degree elements which have come to be regarded as characteristically English.[2]

As teachers, Holst and Vaughan Williams insisted on the study of English music of the sixteenth and seventeenth centuries, directing their young students, among them Elizabeth Maconchy, to study folk songs, the madrigalists, and Purcell. With a tradition thus assimilated and reaffirmed, the composers born in the first decades of the twentieth century were able to begin the task of reintegrating the national music with assimilated contemporary developments in Europe.

At the same time some observers would say that this reawakening to things English was fine and good but so very late in comparison to events and musical movements on the Continent. Composer Denis ApIvor describes the British music in the early 1920s as follows:

> The difficulty in writing about the post-war period, or indeed about British music of any period, is the combination of blinkered non-conformity and "time-compression" which characterises the island scene. Vaughan Williams and his school belong to the modern era, yet they exhibit the bizarre phenomena of a school of folk-song "nationalists" functioning about half a century after the epic folk-song schools of Russia and Central Europe had shot their bolts, and contemporaneously with the "revolutionary" Schoenberg, Webern, Stravinsky.[3]

One can see that provincialism and complacency were not easy barriers to overcome, and it was not easy for some composers to push through the "mists created by the foggy dew of the Renaissance of British Music."[4] Andrew Porter put it this way:

> The wide British public has no taste for contemporary music. In the opera house it goes regularly to a handful of works from Mozart to Puccini, in the concert hall from Bach to early Stravinsky. It has no national pride, and when a composer dies he is forgotten (last year there was but a single performance of Vaughan Williams symphony in London's Festive Hall). This is the steady background; foreground figures come and go, for as Delius remarked in 1912, "the English like vogues for this and that. Now Sibelius, and when they're tired of him they'll boost up Bruckner and Mahler." In fact it took about fifty years (and Sibelius' death) for Bruckner and Mahler to oust Sibelius from the public's favor—and then the ousting was complete. This "vogue" aspect of English musical life (which involves performers too) is an important, distasteful, and often unhealthy fea-

ture of English musical life. Its movements are unpredictable. Interest does not endure.[5]

This was the dilemma facing the emerging group of young composers in the 1930s, which included Edmund Rubbra, William Walton, Lennox Berkeley, Priaulx Rainier, Constant Lambert, Alan Rawsthorne, Grace Williams, Michael Tippett, Elisabeth Lutyens, Benjamin Britten, and Elizabeth Maconchy. It was the dilemma not only of the unknown composer but also of the contemporary composer, attempting to admit and integrate a more international style into a personal language, thus moving away from the provincialism that had characterized British schooling and composition.

The revival of the British choral tradition in the early twentieth century is one of many factors that fueled the English Musical Renaissance. The Tudor revival affected the composers mentioned, all of whom composed noteworthy choral works. For the first time, performing editions of works by Tye, Tallis, Taverner, Byrd, Morley, and Dowland, transcribed from part-books, became available. Polyphonic works of the Tudor period were the exact opposite of what had become the norm in Victorian music, where the melody was in the highest voice; the bass part was static; the texture was chordal; the rhythmic patterns consisted of two, three, and four beats in a bar; and the words of the text were made to fit the music. In Tudor music, the interest was evenly distributed between the various voices, and even the basses shared melodic interest with a texture that was primarily polyphonic. Lines were conceived horizontally, but chordal texture was found as well. Rhythmic patterns were usually irregular; cross accents added rhythmic interest. Words were paramount—they inspired and shaped the music. The first editions of *Tudor Church Music*, *The English Madrigal School*, and the *Collected Works of William Byrd* were now readily obtainable and served as models for works in which mixed textures were used, sensitivity to text-setting was heightened, and interest in the a cappella tradition was reestablished.

The Tudor revival and the awakening of interest in English folk song happened simultaneously. Cecil Sharp and Vaughan Williams, the leaders in the folk music resurgence, spent time collecting songs from rural communities. "Folk song shared certain characteristics (irregular phrases, rhythmic variation, use of modes, and even certain melodic devices) with Tudor music and so reinforced the latter's influence."[6]

Vaughan Williams and Gustav Holst rebelled against eighteenth- and nineteenth-century conventions and yet made no attempt to forge a new music, as did Debussy, Schoenberg, Bartók, and Stravinsky. Vaughan Williams in particular looked to the past and found inspiration in both Tudor and folk music:

Instead of inventing new scales and systems he achieved release by returning to the ancient modes. By applying to modal idioms the techniques and resources of a forward-looking contemporary composer, his music formed a bridge across the centuries; yet so strong was his musical personality that these disparate elements of ancient and modern became fused into a style which was not only highly personal but also intensely national.[7]

Vaughan Williams' Mass in G is an example of a work connected with the past. Scored for solo quartet and unaccompanied double choir, it was intended for liturgical use. The Mass was "written in response to the revival of Byrd and the English polyphonic school at Westminster Cathedral. The mass broke new ground, setting a standard for the recreation of the a cappella tradition."[8]

In British music history, large choral compositions could always be heard at choral festivals held throughout England. These festivals, where the large-scale works of Handel and Mendelssohn were performed in the nineteenth century, aroused steady interest in the composition of oratorios and other large festal pieces. In 1905 the Leith Festival was founded by Margaret Vaughan Williams, Ralph's sister. At Leith, Vaughan Williams encouraged performances of larger works by young composers, which helped them gain exposure and recognition. Vaughan Williams contributed over fifty compositions to the choral repertoire, including oratorios and cantatas like *Sancta civitas* (1926), *Dona nobis pacem* (1936), and *Hodie* (1954).

Important oratorios composed during the first half of the twentieth century include *Belshazzar's Feast* (1931) by William Walton, which is considered to be the biggest and most important choral piece since Elgar's *Dream of Gerontius*. In *A Child of Our Time* (1941) Michael Tippett incorporated Negro spirituals into his highly sophisticated work. Both Walton and Tippett have composed other works for chorus, and their pieces have achieved prominent positions in choral programming in the United States.

Benjamin Britten, regarded as one of the greatest modern British composers, "was able to look beyond the limited horizons of the self-consciously nationalistic manner that then enjoyed favour in much institutional teaching."[9] Unlike Vaughan Williams, whose interest in folk song became the basis of major elements in his style, Britten's point of departure was the music of Henry Purcell:

> Though Purcell wrote in major and minor keys and was generally diatonic, he treated harmony and part-leading with a freedom which would have been unthinkable a century or even half a century later. It is this freedom within tonal writing that Britten has rediscovered and developed. Whereas nearly all contemporary composers seem to have taken refuge in an idiom derived from Schoenberg and Webern, Britten has remained conservative and is one of the few who is still in touch with Everyman.[10]

Choral and vocal works dominate Britten's oeuvre after his return from the States in 1942. From his earliest choral work, "A Boy Was Born," which dates back to 1933, when it was premiered at the Macnaghten-Lemare Concerts, Britten placed great importance on the text. This concern and sensitivity to text-setting

can be seen in his operas, his works for solo voice, and his forty choral compositions, including *Rejoice in the Lamb, Hymn to St. Cecelia,* and *War Requiem,*
which were so popular and warmly received by American audiences.

Other composers of this generation, who have composed viable choral works
include Lennox Berkeley, a pupil of Nadia Boulanger; Edmund Rubbra, a student
of Gustav Holst; Elisabeth Lutyens, who studied with Harold Darke; and Grace
Williams, Elizabeth Maconchy, and Constant Lambert, who were pupils of Ralph
Vaughan Williams.

Foundations and Forebears

In the early decades of the twentieth century, several people and new organizations
laid the foundations on which young composers were able to build. Dame Ethel
Smyth was always heralded as the exception to the rule as far as women composers
were concerned:

> Generally speaking, the remark *Mulier taceat in musica* holds good, in spite of
> the many ladies who are occupied with musical needlework, sewing melodies,
> and knitting tones. All this is imitation work after good masters. But there is
> one, an English woman, who has swept away, I had almost said, battered down
> such prejudices. Her name is Ethel Smyth.[11]

From the beginning, Smyth was independent and chose to seek out her train-
ing in Germany, although both the Royal College of Music and the Royal Academy of Music were coeducational institutions. She had many performances abroad
before any at home, and she was in the forefront of musical life, attempting to
win performances not only because she was a contemporary composer but also
because she was a woman composer. Her response to the attention she was finally getting on the pages of the *Musical Times* is revealing:

> I am much gratified at your devoting so much space in your last two numbers to
> me. In view of the appreciation the Press of this country has recently shown me,
> and still more perhaps given the testimony from abroad, in which temptation to
> an over-favorable estimate of home produce cannot play a part, it may surprise
> you to hear that no single composition of mine has ever been performed at any
> British Festival though I regularly implore for even a bare ten minutes.[12]

Henry J. Wood, sole conductor of the Promenade Concerts that were enjoyed
by so many between 1895 and 1941, was an important early champion of new
music. He conducted works by Debussy, Skryabin, and Bartók, and he urged
those playing Schoenberg's *Five Pieces for Orchestra* under him to "stick to it,
gentlemen, this is nothing to what you'll have to play in twenty-five years time."[13]
Wood did a great deal to promote young British composers and performers, and
the Proms became a central feature of British musical life. Elizabeth Maconchy's

first performance of *The Land* in England was conducted by Wood at the Proms in 1930.

Sir Thomas Beecham championed the operas of Ethel Smyth and gave first performances of her works in Britain. He also presented a number of other new operas in Britain, including works by Russian composers, and was responsible for the first appearances in London of Diaghilev's Ballets Russes.

In August of 1911 an invitational meeting was held to inaugurate an organization called the Society of Women Musicians. Many reasons were enumerated for its founding, not the least of which was that "there was one branch of creative art in which women had no past as they had in literature or painting, but, there was a tremendous future for women in musical composition."[14] The group met regularly, performed concerts of compositions by women, sponsored lectures about various aspects of compositional technique, introduced works by women composers from America, and much more. Dame Ethel Smyth was part of the organization, and in later years, Elizabeth Maconchy was vice president.

In the early 1920s, many young British composers belonged to the International Society for Contemporary Music (ISCM), which was formed in 1922 as a means of breaking down national barriers between composers. The first organization's headquarters were in London, under the presidency of E. J. Dent. Some of Lutyens' and Maconchy's first performances were in early ISCM concerts held all over Europe. Also in 1922, the British Broadcasting Corporation (BBC) was created, and it proved to be a powerful and continuing influence on English musical life. In its early years, the BBC was responsible for exposing English listeners to a wide variety of new music from abroad. Through radio broadcasts many Britons heard performances of Bartók, Stravinsky, Schoenberg, Berg, and Webern for the first time. The BBC Symphony Orchestra, which became a vehicle for the performance of many new works, was formed in 1930 and later commissioned works from Maconchy, Lutyens, and Musgrave.

Elisabeth Lutyens, one of the most ingenious and outspoken proponents of new musical trends, wanted a vehicle for hearing her own works and those of her friends. Accordingly, she founded a concert series with two other women, violist Anne Macnaghten and aspiring conductor Iris Lemare. The Macnaghten-Lemare Concerts stirred the musical community by calling attention not just to women but to all living composers because they were all equally neglected. The women's aim was to discover and encourage British composers and to present concerts of contemporary music of differing styles in which British music predominated: "Elisabeth Lutyens brought us together and put the idea that concert works by grossly neglected young British composers might be made to 'sell' if properly presented and carefully cushioned by some works of more senior, established British composers and some seldom heard classical works."[15]

A year later, in September 1932, Vaughan Williams wrote to Anne Macnaghten, "You are doing great work and putting the BBC and T. Beecham to shame."[16] The Macnaghten-Lemare Concerts were consistently reviewed in music journals and newspapers and proved to be an important forum for many young composers:

> Cleverness, vitality, enthusiasm, enterprise—all these and more go to the making of programmes that are packed with interesting new works and admirable performances. Best of all, Miss Macnaghten and Miss Lemare communicate their own intense belief in the worthwhileness of new music to everyone concerned. It is immensely worthwhile to give young composers this fair, natural hearing for their music after it is written, without the discussions that stultify even the impulse to compose.[17]

The extent to which the women were involved in the Macnaghten-Lemare Concerts is striking: the organizers were women, the Macnaghten Quartet was composed entirely of women, and women composers figured prominently in the programs. When asked if this was a deliberate feminist gesture, Anne Macnaghten replied:

> I don't think so. As far as the quartet is concerned I think it just happened like that. And as for the large number of women composers involved in the Concerts, at that time there were a number of very gifted young women writing music, and because they were women they had a rather greater need to try to get a hearing, because it was more difficult for them. And because we were female, we were more inclined to sympathize.[18]

Several of the composers introduced to the public at the Macnaghten Concerts would attain major importance in British music. Lutyens and Maconchy became part of their generation's vanguard, their works being programmed alongside those of Benjamin Britten, Michael Tippett, and William Walton. Embarking on boldly fresh paths, Lutyens and Maconchy wrote with distinctive and individual voices.

The importance of the English Musical Renaissance and the revitalization of the British choral tradition cannot be overestimated. Musicologists have looked back, sometimes with disdain, on the provincialism and resistant shores of England's green and pleasant land. In addition, the various British institutions and individuals dedicated to the performance and promotion of new music of native composers laid the groundwork for the development of a recognizably national school. The increased compositional activity, coupled with quality and confidence, generated strength and at the same time established something against which to rebel. It is in this context that the successful compositional careers of Elisabeth Lutyens, Elizabeth Maconchy, and Thea Musgrave were allowed to flourish.

Notes

1. Wilfrid Mellers, *Music and Society* (London: Dennis Dobson, 1946), 155.

2. Edwin Evans, "Modern British Composers," *Musical Times* 60 (January 1919): 10–11.

3. Denis Aplvor, "The Avant-garde: Then and Now," *Composer* 59 (Winter 1977): 19.

4. Elisabeth Lutyens, *A Goldfish Bowl* (London: Faber and Faber, 1972), 69.

5. Andrew Porter, "Some New British Composers," in *Contemporary Music in Europe: A Comprehensive Survey*, ed. by P. H. Lang and Nathan Broder (New York: G. Schirmer, 1965), 12–13.

6. Kenneth R. Long, *The Music of the English Church* (London: Hodder and Stoughton, 1971), 423.

7. Long, *The Music of the English Church*, 425.

8. *The New Grove Dictionary of Music and Musicians*, s.v. "Ralph Vaughan Williams," by Hugh Ottaway.

9. *The New Grove Dictionary of Music and Musicians*, s.v. "Benjamin Britten," by Peter Evans.

10. Long, *The Music of the English Church*, 431.

11. Richard Specht, "Dr. Ethel Smyth," *Musical Times* 53 (March 1912): 168.

12. Ethel Smyth, in a letter to the *Musical Times* 53 (April 1912): 232.

13. *The New Grove Dictionary of Music and Musicians*, s.v. "Henry J. Wood," by Ronald Crichton.

14. "Society of Women Musicians," news item in *Musical Times* 52 (August 1911): 535.

15. Ernest Chapman, "The Macnaghten Concerts," *Composer* 57 (Spring 1976): 14.

16. Anne Macnaghten, "The Story of the Macnaghten Concerts," *Musical Times* 100 (1959): 460.

17. M.M.S., "Macnaghten-Lemare Concerts," *Musical Times* 76 (February 1935): 170.

18. Anne Macnaghten, "Anne Macnaghten," *The Strad* 94 (December 1983): 553.

Elisabeth Lutyens (1906-1983)

Agnes Elisabeth Lutyens was born in London on July 9, 1906, the fourth of five children of the distinguished architect Sir Edwin Lutyens and Lady Emily Lytton. Her family was not musical but did not actively disapprove of her interest in music. In fact, Lutyens' introduction to music came when her mother decided that learning the violin would distract Elisabeth from her chronic nail-biting. Soon she began playing the piano as well, finding the solace and solitude she desired.

At fifteen Lutyens began studying violin with Marie Motto, who had her own string quartet that included violist and composer Frank Bridge. At her teacher's concerts Lutyens became acquainted with the string quartet repertoire that she came to love. Motto in turn suggested that Lutyens study piano with Polyxena Fletcher, whom Lutyens later named "the greatest single influence in my life."[1] Although lessons lasted long hours, they seemed timeless, and the two discussed music from the widest and most all-embracing points of view. When Fletcher discovered Lutyens' interest in composition, she started to teach her harmony. At the same time Lutyens began to attend the Proms Concerts, where exposure to the orchestral music of Debussy and Ravel awakened a desire to go to Paris to study. At sixteen she entered the École Normale, studying harmony, solfège, and piano, and there she soaked in as much of the music and culture going on around her as possible.

In 1923 she returned to London, not because she was disenchanted with her Parisian studies, but because she yearned to spend time with her "distant and beloved" mother.[2] Throughout her life, Elisabeth desperately sought the love and affection of her mother, whom she greatly loved and admired. It was this desire that led to an unfortunate interruption in her musical life. Lady Emily was a devoted disciple of Krishnamurti, a controversial world teacher in the Theosophy movement. Although Elisabeth was resentful of the attention Krishnamurti demanded from her mother, she ignored her feelings of skepticism about his mentorship and spent nine months accompanying her mother and Krishnamurti to a variety of locations in Europe and the East. The result, for Elisabeth, was a serious nervous breakdown.

Hoping to resume a more normal life, Lutyens returned to London and entered the Royal College of Music, where she was assigned to Harold Darke.[3] Along with helpful mentorship, Darke assisted in arranging student performances of her works, thus enabling her to grow as a composer.

From this point Lutyens became deeply committed to her craft. At the Royal College of Music she studied viola and piano, sang contralto in the chorus, and applied herself to composition studies. Yet despite the richness of her musical education, Lutyens felt restricted by the conservative musical style advocated at the school. As a result, she developed the strong feelings that enabled her to find her own voice.

During her student years Lutyens met people with whom she would be associated for a long time—some she loved: Alan Rawsthorne, Constant Lambert, William Walton, Elizabeth Maconchy, Iris Lemare, and Anne Macnaghten; and some she detested: Michael Tippett and Benjamin Britten. To Anne Macnaghten, in particular, Lutyens would complain that there was no forum for the promotion of new music, especially new music by women. Lutyens had sent several scores to the BBC, but they were returned unopened, which only fueled her cynicism. Soon she and Macnaghten decided to design a platform for performances of works by their contemporaries. The result was the distinguished Macnaghten-Lemare Concert Series, which continues at the time of this printing. In the words of Iris Lemare:

> Our origin was strictly realistic, not altruistic. Three young women musicians found sex discrimination blocking all progress for them: Elisabeth Lutyens as as composer, myself as a conductor, and Anne Macnaghten with a string quartet to launch.[4]

With these forces and this philosophy, the Macnaghten-Lemare Concert Series began.

The early 1930s marked other important firsts in Lutyens' life, including her first important public performance. Her ballet *The Birthday of the Infanta* (1932) was conducted by her friend Constant Lambert. Gradually during the 1930s her works reached audiences through the London Contemporary Music Centre (LCMC), her own Macnaghten Concerts, or the Adolph Hallis Concerts, which arranged the premiere of her first string quartet. Later, she was regularly featured in LCMC programs, starting in 1939, when her second string quartet was played at the Warsaw International Society for Contemporary Music (ISCM) Festival. Of her early efforts, the Sonata for Viola Op. 5, No. 4 (1938), the second string quartet Op. 5, No. 5 (1939), and the String Trio Op. 5, No. 6 (1939) were the only ones that Lutyens allowed to stand in the canon of her works. Excellently conceived for their forces, they are highly chromatic, taut, and original in structure, but there is little indication here of the sound world of the Concerto Op. 8, No. 1 for Nine Instruments of 1940.

In 1933 Lutyens married Ian Glennie, a singer who had studied at the Royal College of Music. The fruits of this otherwise unsuccessful marriage were three children: Sebastian and twins Rose and Theresa. Although this period was fallow for her as a composer, several discoveries proved inspirational and gave her a new perspective. One important experience was her introduction to the Purcell fantasias for viols, which she said led her to discover serial composition. These works by Purcell, harmonically bold, seemed to Lutyens to be more modern than many other works by Purcell, and her attempt to organize atonal musical conceptions in accordance with this indigenous tradition of viol fantasias gave birth to a twelve-tone theme. Another revelatory experience was hearing a performance of Webern's "Das Augenlicht" in 1938. A year earlier she had heard the same composer's *Bagatelles* and *Five Pieces for Orchestra*, and thought this music the most thrilling she had heard in recent years.

The Chamber Concerto No. 1 for Nine Instruments, her most innovative work of the period, marks the beginning of a new musical language that developed naturally out of the rigor of her compositional attitudes and her fascination with mathematical relationships. Yet she had already shown a full understanding of Webern in her String Trio of the previous year. In these works Lutyens moved away decisively from Britain's musical mainstream, and her voice became "for many years, a lone one crying in a particularly lonely wilderness."[5]

A figure who buoyed Lutyens in this transitional time was Edward Clark, who played many roles in her life. During the 1930s Lutyens had noticed Clark's name in conjunction with nearly every new music concert, performance, festival, and society, and she finally had the opportunity to meet him at a party at the home of composer Alan Rawsthorne. In 1940 Lutyens ended her marriage to Ian Glennie and went to live with Clark in London. They were married in 1941, beginning a successful personal and professional partnership that lasted until Clark's death in 1961.

Edward Clark has gone largely unrecognized in twentieth-century Britain. Lutyens devoted several chapters in *A Goldfish Bowl* to Clark's accomplishments, and she continued to feel bitter that this man remained invisible to the general public.[6] Recent historians have begun to give credit to Clark, whose enormous influence on the programming of the BBC from the early 1920s until 1936 resulted in the presentation of much contemporary music at the network. As early as 1921, when Schoenberg's Chamber Symphony and String Quartet No. 2 and Stravinsky's *A Soldier's Tale* were introduced in London, Clark's advocacy of contemporary music in general, and of the Second Viennese School in particular, had brought both Schoenberg and Stravinsky to the BBC. In his book *BBC Symphony Orchestra*, Nicholas Kenyon notes the easy, close relationship Clark sustained with most of the important conductors and composers of the day. Letters survive to Clark from Ansermet ("Dear old Boy"), Bartók, Bax, Berg, Berkeley, Lord Berners, Britten, Casella, Coates, Dallapiccola, Delius, Dent, van Dieren, Falla,

Gerhard, Hindemith, Ireland, Kodály, Koussevitzky, Lambert, Malipiero, Milhaud, Moeran, Nin, Poulenc, Prokofiev, Veress, Walton, and Webern: a roll call of important musicians of the interwar years.[7]

After leaving the BBC over a disputed change in programming, Clark continued to be an advocate of contemporary music, and he gave constant and committed support to Lutyens.

On September 7, 1940, Lutyens and Clark were on their way to the Proms at Queen's Hall for the performance of Lutyens' Three Orchestral Pieces, Op. 7 (1939) when they were confronted by the first bombs of the full-scale blitz on London. The hall had sold out in advance, but few people actually attended the concert. The concert began and ended; no one remembered what happened. Lutyens and Clark spent the night in Queen's Hall with the orchestra, soloists, and audience.

Life for Lutyens was extremely difficult during and after the war. Neither her former nor her current husband made much money, and Lutyens made a meager living copying music—her first job was copying *Limehouse Blues*. Although her own composing went largely by the board, she said "come what may, I never went to bed without writing a few bars to keep my hand in."[8] Later she obtained orchestral and arranging jobs that interested her more and paid better.

The George, a restaurant in London, became the focal point of Lutyens' social and professional life for some nine years. The friends she made there gave her many opportunities to write music for radio and drama, and she collaborated with Louis MacNeice, Dylan Thomas, and Reggie (R. D.) Smith.

Late in 1944, Lutyens was offered her first complete film, *Jungle Mariners*, to score. Writing music for documentary films proved to be a main source of income throughout her life. She considered it a form of musical journalism and composed music for over one hundred films. In the last years of the 1940s, Lutyens began to refine her style. While she experimented with serial language through the decade, she explored in other areas as well.

The romantic expressionism and the bold dramatic outlines of the Three Symphonic Preludes, for example, contrast strongly with the unrhetorical First Chamber Concerto, while the neo-classical concertos for bassoon and horn are quite different again. Yet with each work Lutyens approached a little nearer the sensibility and style of her maturity. By the end of the war she was using with commanding ease a fully developed 12-note technique: *O Saisons, O Châteaux!* (1946) marked a new important stage in her development.[9]

O Saisons, O Châteaux! is scored for soprano, mandolin, guitar, harp, solo violin, and strings. Setting a poem from Rimbaud's *Les illuminations*, Lutyens creates an extraordinary sense of mood and atmosphere, expressed directly in the beautiful, highly articulate melodic writing that Humphrey Searle considered "the forerunner of her . . . mature style."[10]

The year 1947 saw the composition of two important works. The first was *The Pit*, a dramatic scene for tenor, bass, boy (tacet), women's chorus, and orchestra, commissioned by and dedicated to William Walton. Each of Lutyens' dramatic works is based on either an emotional confrontation or an exposition of contrasting aspects of isolation. For some years, Lutyens was preoccupied with the idea of the victim. In *The Pit*, the feeling of isolation is created by the circumstances of a mining accident. Two men and a boy are entombed; they are the victims, through no fault of their own, of an inescapable situation.[11] Choruses are used as in Greek drama: they comment, observe, threaten, or forewarn, occasionally becoming abstract parts of the musical background. In *The Pit*, the chorus of wailing wives laments in prayerful keening.

The second important composition in 1947 was the viola concerto, a terse, four-movement serial composition. Lutyens avoids application of orthodox twelve-tone technique. Instead, she uses traditional shapes, vertical, diatonic structures, where notes are repeated before the series is complete. The last movement is a passacaglia. Typical of her best works, the themes are clearly presented, the texture is widely spaced, and the form is simple and direct. The viola concerto was performed by the BBC in 1950, and favorably evaluated in the *Music Review*:

> Those of us who know something about twelve-tone technique . . . tend to approach a new dodecaphonic work with well-founded fear, knowing as we do how difficult it is even for a great talent to master this method of composition, and how easy, on the other hand to hide one's lack of inspiration *even from oneself* behind twelve-tone pseudo-esotericism. The first surprise about Lutyens' concerto was . . . that (as the wide and sincerely enthusiastic applause showed) it was not esoteric. . . . Perhaps the thus conservative twelve-tone composer has a special and important historic task: to familiarize the conservative music lover with the new language and to build a bridge between those many pasts and futures which form our bewildering musical present.[12]

The BBC premiered three other works from this fertile period: *Salute for Orchestra* (1945), *Three Symphonic Preludes* (1946), and *Petite Suite* (1947), adapted from the music for the film *Jungle Mariners*. Her Concerto for Horn (1947), dedicated to Dennis Brain, was chosen to be performed by the ISCM in Oslo that year. The Proms selected the *Suite* to be programmed between *Belshazzar's Feast* and *Daphnis and Chloe*. In November of the same year, a concert of her works was performed at the BBC in a series called "Contemporary British Composers."

Another side of Lutyens can be seen in her Stevie Smith songs of 1948. These cabaret songs are light and humorous, and capture in music the essence of Stevie Smith's poetry. They are simple and tonal in style.

In a poignant chapter in *A Goldfish Bowl* titled, simply, "1948," Lutyens describes the breakdown she suffered after the war. Clark was too busy planning concerts and corresponding with composers to write her while she was away at the sanatorium, which only served to increase her anxiety. Money worries and Edward's frustrations, her concern and feelings of responsibility for her children, all served to erode her sense of well-being. Eventually, Lutyens returned to her mother's home until she was strong enough to resume her busy life. Generally, the years from 1948 to 1952 were some of her worst. Edward scarcely communicated with her, and he was contributing nothing financially. Her four children (now including

Conrad, born to Lutyens and Clark) were assigned to various family members for support. She was drinking heavily and wrote music only for radio and six documentary films. During this time, under the influence of alcohol and what she considered bad advice from friends, she left Edward and attempted to lead an independent life. Clark promptly suffered a heart attack from which he recovered, and which served to secure their relationship until his death nine years later. Feeling that alcohol was taking over her life, she entered a treatment program with a recommended doctor and overcame the desire to drink, at least for quite some time.

With these tumultuous events behind her, 1953 seemed to mark a change. At forty-seven, Lutyens solidified elements in her compositional style and emerged, with her String Quartet No. 6, a mature composer. Marks of her mature style include the use of palindrome structures, a progressive paring down of materials and gestures, and a greater balance and economy in her use of musical material. There is consistency in her harmonic language and an overall tightening of organization. Her approach to composition is rigorous. She exhibits a natural instinct to keep the music varied. Her music is impressive when it involves voices; both solo vocal and choral works are characterized by a wide-ranging choice of texts, as well as by her sensitive, musical reaction to the words themselves.

Lutyens wrote the String Quartet No. 6 in a single twelve-hour sitting. Speaking once about her dedication of the work to the painter Francis Bacon, Lutyens compared her method of composition with the artist's tendency to work very quickly when he wanted to make a great, nervous impact. Lutyens herself was able to compose with great speed and get results, one outcome of her extensive experience writing scores for films. When a critic accused her of being quite prolific, she retorted that a dog barks and a composer composes.

The sixth quartet is in two movements (124 measures). In comparison to her earlier chamber works, the quartet's rhythm has become freer, the parts have become more independent, ingenious, and complex, and the compression of thought is greater. The slow movement (marked *adagio, molto legato*, and *senza espressione, pianissimo*) is followed by a restatement of the first movement (marked *allegro moderato*). One writer compares the compositional technique to "her stream of musical consciousness," which "places much reliance on a continuously evolving thread of melody."[13]

As in the early 1930s, when Lutyens helped initiate the Macnaghten Concerts, in 1953 she founded another organization: Composer's Concourse. She conceived it as a forum for composers to meet and discuss their technical problems and to discover what others were writing. She thought this might help end her own isolation as well as that of others. Lutyens, with John Amis, Lennox Berkeley, Alan Bush, Ernest Chapman, Arnold Cooke, and Eileen Ralf, planned two or three series of talks during a year, each followed by a general discussion.[14]

Lutyens wrote fifteen choral works between 1954 and 1979.[15] Nine are unaccompanied, and eight of these are settings for SATB choir. *The Hymn of Man*, originally set for men's chorus in 1965, was rescored by the composer for SATB in 1970. Six works are accompanied, four by large orchestral forces. *Counting Your*

Steps (1972) features four flutes and four percussionists. The choral works vary in length from the five-minute *Sloth—One of the Seven Deadly Sins* (1974) to the forty-minute *De Amore* (1957).

Lutyens' selection of texts is rich and varied. Most are in English, and there are some translations. *Counting Your Steps*, for example, was translated from Pygmy poetry. Lutyens also felt comfortable working in German and French, as when she set sections from Austrian philosopher Ludwig Wittgenstein's *Logisch-Philosophische Abhandlung* and Rimbaud's *Les illuminations*. Lutyens is the author of several of her own texts. Only two of fifteen choral works feature sacred texts: *Magnificat and Nunc Dimittis* (1965) from the Gospel according to Luke, for unaccompanied chorus; and *Encomion* (1963) from Ecclesiasticus, for chorus and brass. Other authors set by Lutyens include Chaucer, Byron, Yeats, Swinburne, Petrarch, Conrad, Donne, and Wordsworth. Her choral works of the 1950s and 1960s generally are conceived for larger forces than those of the 1970s, most of which are written for chamber ensembles. An exception is *Voice of Quiet Waters* (1972), which is set for full orchestra, soloists, and chorus.

Requiem for the Living

Lutyens withdrew seventeen choral works from her canon, seven accompanied and ten unaccompanied, many from her student days.[16] Her reasons for withdrawing *Requiem for the Living*, finished in 1948 and performed and broadcast in 1952 by the BBC, are not known. Perhaps it was because the work was not exclusively serial and Lutyens wished to be known as a twelve-tone composer. In addition, it might have been too personal a work. Certainly, it is not as taut as her later compositions, and it sounds like a dramatic scena, akin to her writing for film. Perhaps she feared that if people heard her more tonal music, they would ignore the more difficult twelve-tone music for which she wished to be known.

Requiem for the Living is a nonliturgical setting of the Requiem, with a text by Lutyens. There is no doubt Lutyens was familiar with Brahms' nonliturgical Requiem or Hindemith's *When Lilacs Last in the Door-yard Bloom'd*. It has been said that Brahms conceived of his Requiem as a consolation for the living rather than the traditional Mass for the dead. Lutyens wrote hers for the tired, those people chained to their duties, the discontented. It is beseeching and sympathetic. There is no judgment involved. It is positive, hopeful, and encouraging: a tribute to life. Perhaps the work is autobiographical.[17]

As in many other more familiar settings of the Requiem, Lutyens writes for four soloists, full orchestra, and SATB chorus. She uses the titles from the traditional sections of the Requiem, and she sometimes adheres to the traditional moods and meanings of individual movements. But at other times she changes and juxtaposes completely opposing meanings, as in the first movement for chorus (II), "Requiem Aeternam." The original text of the *Missa pro defunctis* appeals to God: give rest unto them, hear my prayer, all flesh shall come to thee. While retaining the customary musical mood—a prayerful, hushed *pianissimo*—Lutyens opens her movement, full of quiet joy, to the text: "Breathe in us, life, and breathing let us live," then gradually builds dynamically to "a lively wakefullness." Four measures later, Lutyens concludes the movement on a major-major seventh chord on the word "breathe."

In the opening of the traditional sequence, "Dies Irae" (Day of Wrath), the element of judgment prevails, and musical settings are generally agitated and forceful, with strongly marked rhythmic figures. Lutyens makes no mention of a wrathful God in her text, but rather, with equal musical energy and vigor, depicts a world in chaos, where people are weak and afraid. It is a world gone mad, the world of postwar Europe. With full orchestral forces the movement, marked *poco allegro, fortissimo, feroce e marcato*, maintains tension throughout. Perhaps the closest relationship between Lutyens' setting and the traditional Requiem occurs in the "Benedictus," although Lutyens invokes a different sort of blessing: that of a future filled with "peace and prosperity."

In *Requiem for the Living*, Lutyens uses several methods that were already her trademark to unify the work. One device is a strong, recurring musical-textural passage that appears four times in the course of this thirteen-minute work. The passage opens the first choral movement, closes the work, and stands on either side of the middle movement. The first and final appearances of its text are identical (see Appendix D, lines 1-7), and save for additional orchestral doublings, all musical elements are also the same. When the passage first appears in movement II, mm. 23-37 (see Example 2.1), the chorus is doubled by brass (two horns, two trombones), and flutes enter for three measures to reinforce "alive to a lively wakefullness," mm. 32-34. (In the BBC recording of 1952, the chorus sings mm. 23-37 unaccompanied.) Tenors double basses in ten of fifteen measures (Example 2.1).

Example 2.1. *Requiem for the Living,* mm. 23-37.

In movement VI, m. 106, the music of Example 2.1 is truncated from fifteen measures to seven (mm. 106-112), strings are added, and the first four measures are transposed down a half step. The final three measures of the passage, still doubled by strings and brass, are strikingly dissonant, depicting the world's unrest with clashing chromatic sonorities. The text is slightly altered as the chorus pleads for Prometheus (tenor soloist), "Breathe in him, life though a world's in travail, through a world's unrest" (see Example 2.2).

Example 2.2. *Requiem for the Living*, mm. 106-112.

In movement VII, the passage has been further reduced to four measures. Following the soprano's beseeching solo, which focuses on children's tender years,

the chorus sopranos (divisi) and altos sing unaccompanied, "Breathe on them,
life," transposed up a tritone (see Example 2.3).

Example 2.3. *Requiem for the Living*, mm. 156-159.

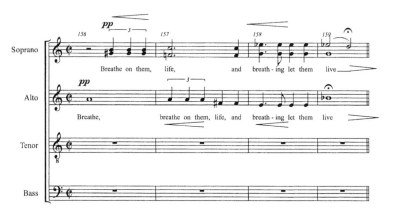

In the final appearance of the passage in movement XII, the first eleven measures reveal musical-textural features identical to those that opened the work. In
m. 226, however, full orchestral forces reinforce the final choral statement, a second alto part is added an octave below the soprano, and a one-measure extension
prolongs the last chord.

As Examples 2.1-2.3 illustrate, occasional tonal references are apparent in
this piece. Although there is no clear tonal center, major triads and their inversions
appear randomly throughout the work. Also evident is the unfolding of all twelve
pitches in the opening four measures of Example 2.1. In Example 2.2, m. 110, all
twelve pitches are used in three chords (twelve-note aggregates); each chord in m.
111 uses the same pitches, but the chords are voiced differently from those in m.
110. These twelve-note melodic and harmonic structures occur frequently throughout the work and lend coherence to the whole, but they are not used consistently.
Although sections of all movements in this work make use of serial techniques, it
is not a dodecaphonic work.

The first and solely instrumental movement, where most of the building material appears, contains two twelve-note musical themes and one twelve-note aggregate, the same aggregate as in Example 2.2 above. The work opens with an E^b
pedal, sustained in the bassoons and double basses for twenty-two measures, reminiscent of the opening of Wagner's opera *Das Rheingold*. The first twelve-note
theme appears in mm. 4-5 and again in m. 20 (Example 2.4). The same theme and
the twelve-note aggregate recur no fewer than four times in the course of the piece;
one other twelve-note series and aggregate are used as well. Yet many sections of
the work are freely composed and do not use material related to these structures.

Example 2.4. *Requiem for the Living*, mm. 1-6.

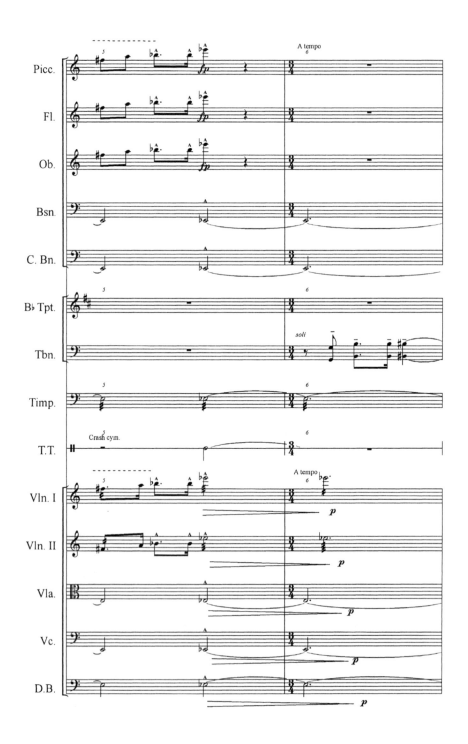

Though written before the formation of Lutyens' mature style, the *Requiem* reveals many familiar features of her writing. In keeping with her desire for balance and economy of musical material, Lutyens uses the full orchestra as though it were a chamber ensemble, rarely employing all forces at the same time. However, in the "Dies Irae," "Offertorium," and "Sanctus," all instruments play in unison. Orchestral doubling is common in other choral sections, and scoring is sparse in the three movements for orchestra alone.

In three of the four movements for solo voices, the orchestral support is minimal; only the movement for tenor calls for the full complement of players. The tenor, recounting the tale of the unhappy fate of Prometheus, spins out a disjunct line (Example 2.5). The chorus responds, as in a Passion, and entreats, "Breathe in him, life, and living let him breathe, though a world's in travail, through a world's unrest."

Example 2.5. *Requiem for the Living*, mm. 95-105.

Winds, brass, and strings punctuate every measure of the tenor's solo, in stark contrast to the more exposed movements for mezzo, soprano, and baritone, which have barely an orchestral whisper for accompaniment. These soloists sing recitative-like phrases with repeated-note passages and intricate rhythms. In addition, the soprano and mezzo parts contain challenging chromatic intervals and angular lines depicting the pain or pity of the child and the mother. The choral writing, by comparison, is conjunct, in a comfortable range and a reasonable tessitura. There are no complex rhythmic changes or unusual meters to accommodate the text. The choral writing is almost exclusively homophonic, with several unison passages interspersed. In her *Requiem for the Living* Lutyens has written a short, dramatic choral work with a poignant message, one that is approachable for all forces involved. Only the lack of a readily available edition keeps it from receiving the public performances it deserves.

Motet (Excerpta Tractati Logico-Philosophici)

It is generally agreed that the *Motet (Excerpta Tractati Logico-Philosophici)*, Opus 27 (1953), is one of Lutyens' most remarkable compositions. Analyzing this piece in some depth will reveal compositional techniques found in many of her works. For her text Lutyens selected a series of remarks from Ludwig Wittgenstein's *Logisch-Philosophische Abhandlung* (1912),[18] a seventy-five-page tract that poses the question: How is language possible? How can a person, by uttering a sequence of words, say something? And how can another person understand? The formal, abstract nature of the text frees Lutyens from necessity of interpreting the words in a literal manner. One can take any of the individual propositions from the text—such as "facts in logical space are the world," "logic fills the world," "the world and life are one," or "in the world everything is as it is and happens as it does happen"—and one would have a precise picture of the music itself. For example, the line "in the world everything is as it is and happens as it does happen" presents an order of things. Wittgenstein starts out seemingly dry and factual but ends with a sense of the inexplicable, illogical, and unanswerable aspects of the world. One can break life down into questions and answers, but the fact is that "eternal life" is enigmatic: on the one hand, logic fills the world, and on the other hand, "nothing can be understood." It is a riddle, and even the riddle does not exist.

Since Lutyens is modeling her work on Wittgenstein's tract, she is freed from the need to interpret, since the mapping itself provides a significant transfer of information.[19] By setting a model of the tract in the music itself (the tract is the Wittgenstein text, the model is Lutyens' understanding of the philosophical meaning as it relates to the musical meaning), the relationship inherent in the tract is automatically subsumed into the music:

world = music (motet)
facts = twelve-note aggregates
atomic fact = aggregate
logical = analytical/theoretical
object = note
space = pitch
time = time
color = timbre

The world is everything that is the case.
(Music is everything that is the case.)
The world is the totality of facts.
(Music is the totality of twelve-note aggregates.)
Facts in logical space are the world . . .

(Twelve-note aggregates, analyzed pitches, are the music . . .)
An atomic fact is a combination of objects.
(An aggregate is a combination of notes.)
Objects form the substance of the world.
(Notes form the substance of the music.)

If one substitutes the words in the left column for those in the right, the mapping is clear: both tracts work.

Lutyens' motet, then, is not a setting of words so much as a realization of Wittgenstein's philosophical ideas through her technique of musical composition. Familiar features of a Renaissance motet are immediately recognizable: imitation, inversion, paired imitation, free contrapuntal writing, and contrasting textures and timbres. Renaissance composers also paid attention to the way words were set—successive phrases of text were often set to overlapping points of imitation. In addition, especially with Josquin, the humanistic spirit was reflected in the careful choice of texts.

Whereas Lutyens' motet most definitely uses twelve-tone aggregates, combinations, and serial techniques, it is not dodecaphonic in the classical sense of the word.[20] Lutyens derives the whole piece from two trichords (0, 1, 4) and (0, 3, 4).[21] In analyzing this work using the integer model of pitch, each chromatic pitch class is labeled with an ascending integer. Thus, if C=0, then C#=1, D=2, and B=11. The trichord (0, 1, 4) can be used to describe C, C#, E, or B, C, E♭, etc.[22] In mm. 1-6 (Example 2.6), the first three alto notes are D, D♭, F (2, 1, 5) and the first three tenor notes are C, B, E♭ (0, 11, 3); both of these are permutations of (0, 1, 4).

Example 2.6. *Motet*, mm. 1-6.

The first three notes of the bass are F, D♭, D (5, 1, 2), and the opening three notes of the soprano are E♭, B, C (3, 11, 0), permutations within the trichords of alto and tenor.

Lutyens derives whole rows organically from various permutations of the trichord (0, 1, 4). In Example 2.6, these permutations can be seen on three different levels: permutations within the trichords (0, 1, 4) and (0, 3, 4), where the trichord identity is maintained; permutations in the order of trichords; and permutations of hexachords so that hexachord two is a retrograde inversion or an inversion of hexachord one at any two levels. Trichords might be mixed up or might appear in a strict ordering within the hexachord. Hexachord B, as it appears in the opening measures in the tenor part (0, 11, 3, 7, 8, 4), is a retrograde of hexachord A found in the opening alto line (2, 1, 5, 9, 10, 6). In Example 2.7 below, Lutyens has reversed the order of the trichords. Figure 2.1 shows how Lutyens uses the integer model of pitch in the opening fifteen measures.

Example 2.7. *Motet*, mm. 11-13.

Figure 2.1. *Motet*, mm. 1-15, using an integer model of pitch.

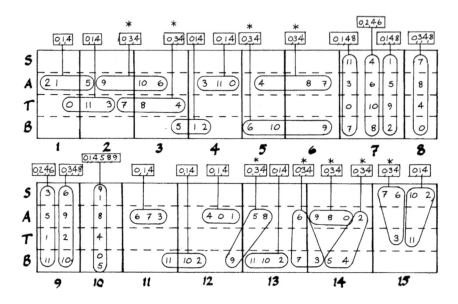

Both hexachords, A and B, when put in normal order, spell (0, 1, 4, 5, 8, 9). This hexachord is all-combinatorial, described as Level 3 in Rahn (see Note 20) and as such exhibits some interesting properties. First, the complement (2, 3, 6, 7, 10, 11), when transposed up a whole step (T2), equals (4, 5, 8, 9, 0, 1) or (0, 1, 4, 5, 8, 9). Second, as already mentioned, Lutyens uses (0, 1, 4) and its inversion (0, 3, 4) as generating cells of the piece. The hexachord, when divided in two, produces (0, 1, 4) and (0, 3, 4). What is interesting is that the hexachord can be divided arbitrarily at any point and achieve the same results: (0, 1, 4), (5, 8, 9), (1, 4, 5), (8, 9, 0), (4, 5, 8), or (9, 0, 1). This extreme example of symmetry explains why it is so easy for Lutyens to move smoothly from one hexachord type to another. Modulation to other hexachords can be done by simple transposition. Third, a property that goes hand in hand with number two is that the hexachord is identical along three axes of symmetry: (0, 1, 4, 5, 8, 9) is intervallically identical to (4, 5, 8, 9, 0, 1). Lutyens is not the only one to have noticed this property. Other twentieth-century composers who have used this hexachord in a nonserial fashion are Bartók in the Bartók scale, and Messiaen in the mode of limited transposition.

Finally, based on properties two and three, the transposition or inversion of the hexachord will produce four and only four such hexachords: (0, 1, 4, 5, 8, 9), (1, 4, 5, 8, 9, 0), (2, 5, 6, 9, 10, 1), and (3, 6, 7, 10, 11, 2). These hexachords relate to the original in one of three ways: (1) all notes are the same; (2) three notes are the same and three notes form the augmented triad (0, 4, 8); and (3) no notes are the same—the hexachord produced is the complement to the first. Other compositions based on this all-combinatorial hexachord are Webern's *Cantata II* and Schoenberg's *Ode to Napoleon Buonaparte.*

Lutyens works in regions and uses her trichords and hexachords in a sectional manner (Example 2.8). Thus, when she starts to use a new technique, she always finishes with the previous one, and she always completes a twelve-note aggregate.

Example 2.8. *Motet,* mm. 117-130.

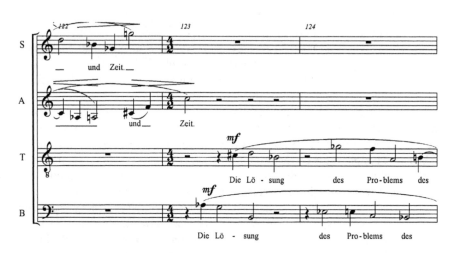

Lutyens uses strict contrapuntal writing in which explicit use of hexachords is immediately apparent. Sometimes she uses vertical stacking—in which case the hexachords are less obvious. There are regions in between—in transition—where no strict linear passage or vertical sonority is immediately recognizable. One can account for practically every pitch. If one were able to take a statistical sampling, each pitch would appear in equal number.

One of the unusual features used in this work has been labeled the "wrong note" procedure. For long periods of time every pitch can be accounted for. Occasionally, however, a "wrong note" appears, as in m. 47 (Example 2.9), at the cadence on "Welt," where C# should be a B.

Example 2.9. *Motet*, m. 47.

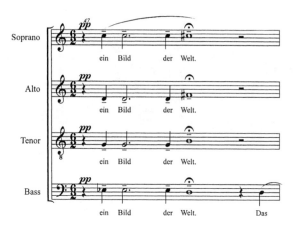

In mm. 54-55 (Example 2.10), Lutyens switches two notes in the alto and tenor voices, a *Stimmtausch*-like effect, probably to achieve the sound she desired rather than the sonority resulting from the established order she has created. Sometimes "wrong notes" can occur because Lutyens juxtaposes a linear pitch and a vertical stacking of pitches and has to make a decision to comply with the dictates of the chord. In Example 2.11, the row begins in m. 76; its twelfth note should be A^b (8) but is notated as F (5) because that pitch fits into the vertical structure.

Example 2.10. *Motet*, mm. 54-55.

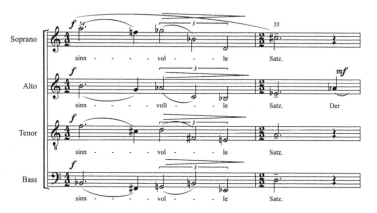

Example 2.11. *Motet*, mm. 76-78.

If such "wrong notes" occurred more frequently, one might question the procedure. However, such notes usually occur at structural points for specific purposes. Lutyens alternates between linear and vertical uses of pitches throughout the piece. Use of the hexachord as a vertical sonority usually signals the approach of a cadence.

Lutyens uses palindromic structures on three different levels. At the beginning, in m. 4 (Example 2.6), palindromes can be seen within the trichords themselves and in the order of trichords. In mm. 27-29 (Example 2.12), a hexachordal palindrome occurs in the bass (9, 1, 0, 8, 4, 5) and alto (5, 4, 8, 0, 1, 9), and at the same time in the tenor (10, 6, 7, 11, 3, 2) and the soprano (2, 3, 11, 7, 6, 10). (In mm. 50-53, the same row appears at four transpositional levels, heard as points of imitation.)[23] In mm. 25-30 the palindromes are exclusively at the same level. This is a conscious compositional decision.

Example 2.12. *Motet*, mm. 25-30.

In the vertical tetrachord aggregates in the motet, Lutyens uses (0, 1, 4, 8), (0, 2, 4, 6), and (0, 1, 4, 8) again. This seems to belie her exclusive use of the (0, 1, 4)-type trichord; however, on closer examination one sees this is not true, as demonstrated in Figure 2.2.

Figure 2.2. Trichord and tetrachord relationships to the row.

```
┌ 0, 1, 4,┐      ┌ 0, 3, 4,┐      ┌ 0, 3, 4,┐      ┌ 0, 1, 4,┐
  8,  9,  0,       4,  1,  5,       3,  7,  6,       2, 10,  11
└ 0, 1, 4, 8, ┘   └ 0, 2, 4, 6, ┘  └ 0, 1, 4, 8, ┘
```

Lutyens uses harmonies as symmetrically as she does linear intervallic relationships within linear twelve-note aggregates. The motet contains several long
periods of tetrachordal parallel motion, where Lutyens maintains aggregates in
clumps. In mm. 113-115 (Example 2.13) Lutyens creates an unusual twist when
she takes the vertical stacks and skews them.

Example 2.13. *Motet*, mm. 113-116.

It is interesting to note that the closest recurrence of the first twelve-note
series (2, 1, 5, 9, 10, 6, 4, 8, 7, 3, 11, 0), from mm. 1-2, occurs two measures
beyond the Golden Mean of the piece, in mm. 96-99. The series is given to the first
soloist in the piece, a soprano, and one note is missing. The unencumbered row
does not occur again until it is stated by the chorus sopranos in mm. 147-151, the
final four measures of the piece. At this point too, the bass states a retrograde
inversion of the same series. Within the 151 measures of the motet, there are occasional free sections in which Lutyens takes liberties with her material, though never
violating the spirit of the (0, 1, 4) sonorities.

The motet is sectional, a patchwork to complement Wittgenstein's propositions, a series of remarks; sometimes sections of text overlap, as do musical sections. The text-setting illustrates another technique that Lutyens absorbed from
earlier Renaissance masters, that of parody. The piece is syllabic throughout. There
is no repetition of text, and phrases are relatively short. In some sections, the vocal

writing is conjunct and lyrical, while other passages are disjunct and angular. There are few extremes of range for the chorus, but the bass part extends over two octaves and is extremely demanding. The SATB soloists in this unaccompanied, ten-minute work have several measures each, the longest and most taxing ones for soprano.

A few specific examples of text-painting can be seen when the piece opens, with the alto and tenor parts only a half step apart. Gradually the other voices join, and the range increases, until all six parts exceed three octaves on the world "Welt." Initially the text states, "The world is everything," and, as more space is encompassed by notes on the page, the text continues, "Facts in logical space are the world." The word "Welt" (world) occurs six times at cadential points and is often given significant treatment. For example, in m. 10, it is given a six-note chord (5, 0, 4, 8, 1, 9); its complement—the other six notes in the series (3, 11, 7, 10, 2, 6)—occurs in m. 21, at the second appearance of "Welt."

Throughout the motet Lutyens uses an extremely small amount of motivic material, yet her formalism and economy do not interfere with her musicality. She has written a taut, complex, lyrical motet, full of choice and craft, and not without the performance difficulties typical of all her works. Her approach is often labeled uncompromising—her critics and some performers say her music is not immediately accessible. Anthony Milner remarks:

> [The motet] is extremely awkward to sing. Months of practice may possibly secure an accurate performance, but its vocal lines, with their large leaps and absence of tonal security, can never be felt to be truly choral in style by the singers. This application of dodecaphony runs counter to the strongest native traditions and will therefore hardly be encouraged by those anxious to preserve high standards of singing.[24]

In contrast to Milner, John Alldis responds:

> Whatever the size of the choir, the effect of the music is one of extraordinary beauty and lucidity. I think Lutyens' motet op. 27 is a marvelous example of a perfect relationship of text and music. The intensely poetic, almost religious intensity of the philosophical extracts from Wittgenstein is delivered by flexible and gratifyingly malleable vocal lines, and the special harmonies recall the Webern cantatas.[25]

"Country of the Stars"

According to Lutyens, "Country of the Stars," a part-song for unaccompanied SATB choir, was written in 1956.[26] Its text is a miniature poetic interpretation of the cosmology from Boethius' *The Consolation of Philosophy,* in Chaucer's translation. The *Consolation* had become an influential compendium of classical thought because the original material on which it was based had been lost to the West.

Philosophy, personified as a woman, converts the imprisoned Boethius to the pla-
tonic notion of good: belief in the highest morality despite trials. The existence of
evil is excluded. The discussion in the *Consolation* of free will, destiny, and fortune had a widespread, deep, and lasting effect, especially on Chaucer's thought
and art. Lutyens sets the penultimate book, metre VI, a poem of praise for the good
order of the world, the beauty of the ordered seasons, and the love that holds
everything together. As in *Motet*, the text is philosophical. Chaucer's translation
achieves passion and intensity through restraint and balance of language. Lutyens
reflects this controlled fervor in the shape and design of the music.

Boethius' view of love and nature is manifest in the section Lutyens selected.
Nature is the God-given principle that enters into every object, celestial and terres-
trial, propelling it in a certain direction. Left to itself, each object would pursue its
course independent of all other objects. The universe would be in flux. Moist
things would be separate from dry things, and all divine elements of the universe
would rush together or fly apart in continual warfare. To rescue the universe from
this confusion, the bond of love exists.

Metre VI from *The Consolation of Philosophy* is more like poetry than prose.
Lutyens sets the text in its original order but omits nearly one-third of it. With
craft, and using her keen sense of language, she divides the selection into two
sections, enabling her to use the form A/A^1 in her musical setting. She does have to
make a few rhythmic changes in the music of A^1 to accommodate different syllables and word emphases in the text. Her setting is strophic and syllabic. Example
2.14 illustrates the equivalent measures in the first and second sections, and the
necessary changes made to accommodate the text.

Example 2.14. "Country of the Stars," mm. 36-37, 93-94.

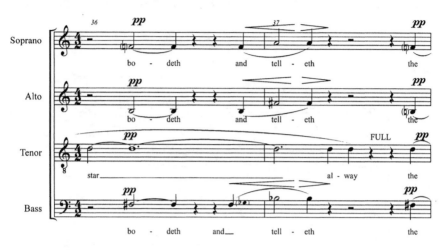

Throughout "Country of the Stars" the half note receives the tactus at a metronome marking of 46. In response to the medieval text, Lutyens chooses the breve as the basic metric unit. There are frequent meter changes—2/2, 3/2, 4/2, 5/2, and 6/2—yet the half-note pulse is constant. Eighth-note motion is a rarity, used twice in choral recitative (mm. 75 and 93) and twice for word emphasis (on "thunderer," m. 8, and "ravishing," m. 92).

A recurring, simple theme opens the piece, entering first in the tenor, and then in soprano, bass, and alto. This material is based on the fundamental set (0, 1, 4) and its congruent set (0, 3, 4), consisting of a minor second and a major third. A second set of entrances follow—S, T, A, B—outlining the interval of a minor sixth and using only the (0, 4, 8) trichord —the augmented triad (Example 2.15). Although thirds and sixths are the basis of this opening section, the recurring use of melodic minor seconds affects the otherwise sweet sound.

Example 2.15. "Country of the Stars," mm. 1-7.

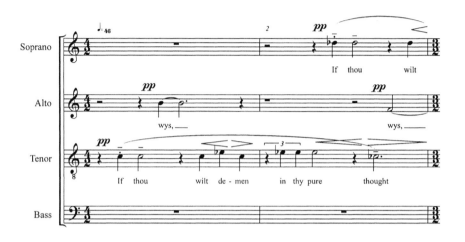

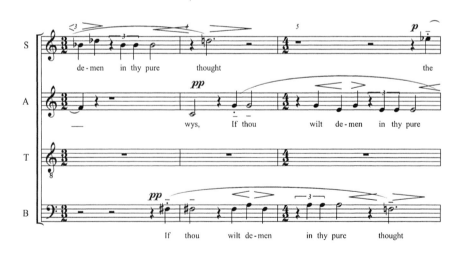

A warmer, more euphonious sound than the opening pattern of thirds and sixths is found in the exposed soprano solo in mm. 25-30 (Example 2.16). The tonal references in the line are audible but fleeting.[27] The line consists of a broken pattern of these sweeter-sounding thirds and sixths, like the interlocking constellations about which the text speaks. The "ravishing courses" of the North Star, the outermost star of Ursa Minor, are described: "abouten the sovereign height of the worlde." At this moment there is a dip of a major seventh down, the first example of the very effective "inverse" word-painting that Lutyens uses several times in this work.

Example 2.16. "Country of the Stars," mm. 25-29.

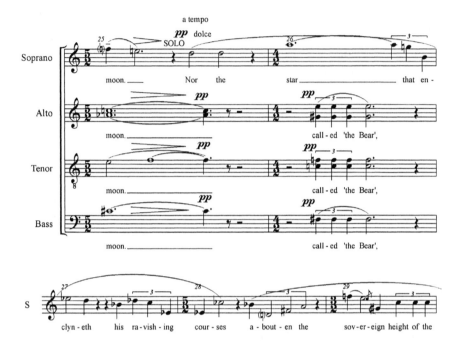

Another example of "inverse" word-painting can be found at the end of each major section of the piece. After a series of dissonant four- and five-note aggregates, the composer restores calm when all voices move to a unison on middle C, *piano*, "thus is discordable battle put out of the country of the stars" (Example 2.17). This use of "inverse" word-painting is a very powerful tool designed to make listeners think.

Example 2.17. "Country of the Stars," mm. 47-54.

Lutyens imaginatively and effectively emphasizes the word "Lucifer," the rising morning star, when she reduces the choral texture and assigns an alto soloist to sing a simple, rising major sixth, in m. 39 (Example 2.18).

Example 2.18. "Country of the Stars," m. 39.

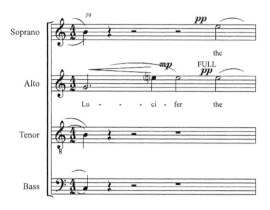

All voice parts include some divisi. Five-voice and six-voice chords appear on important words—"behold," "look," "peace," "star," and "faith." The tessitura of all choral parts is manageable; the soprano part encompasses the greatest range and extends to B♭2. There is some disjunct linear motion in all parts. Major and minor thirds predominate, while the intervals of tritone, fourth, and minor second are also used frequently. Solo voices are used sparingly, emerging gradually from the choral texture and then dissolving back into it (Example 2.19).

Example 2.19. "Country of the Stars," mm. 30-32.

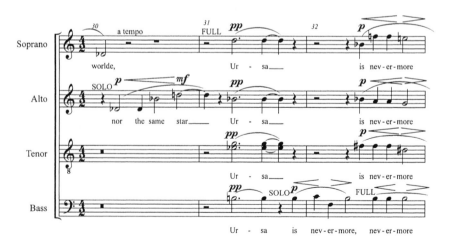

Although "Country of the Stars" is not dodecaphonic, Lutyens uses formal serial procedures. Aggregate formations are used in a controlled manner, although there are no twelve-note aggregates as in the *Motet*. A small number of aggregate structures are used, and they are related to one another as Lutyens deals with the functional relationships of smaller aggregate structures. For example, in the first seven measures (Figure 2.3), one of the most linear sections in the whole work, little is happening on the vertical plane and individual voice parts are conceived horizontally using trichords (0, 1, 4), (0, 3, 4), and (0, 4, 8).

Figure 2.3. "Country of the Stars," mm. 1-7, using an integer model of pitch.

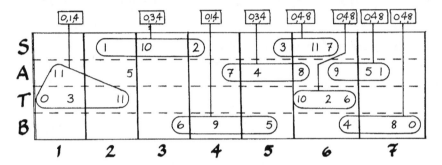

These aggregate structures represent the content of the entire piece. Although the trichords mentioned have the same properties as those in connection with the opus 27 motet, they are used in different ways. (0, 1, 4) and (0, 4, 8) are the building blocks on which the piece is constructed, and almost all aggregates are an outcome of these relationships. In m. 8 Lutyens introduces a third generative sonority: (0, 1, 6, 7).

Both (0, 4, 8) and (0, 6, 7) exhibit interesting symmetrical properties.

T_4 (0, 4, 8)	=	(4-8-0)	=	(0, 4, 8)
T_0I (0, 4, 8)	=	(0-8-4)	=	(0, 4, 8)
T_6 (0, 1, 6, 7)	=	(6-7-0-1)	=	(0, 1, 6, 7)
T_1I (0, 1, 6, 7)	=	(0-11-6-5)	=	(0, 1, 6, 7)

The two kinds of symmetry Lutyens uses are bilateral and rotational (I=bilateral; T=rotational; TI=both; T_0=neither). (0, 4, 8) can combine with any other (0, 4, 8) to create an all-combinatorial hexachord.

(0, 4, 8) + T1 (0, 4, 8)	=	(0, 1, 4, 5, 8, 9)
T_0 (0, 1, 4, 5, 8, 9)	=	(0, 1, 4, 5, 8, 9)
T_2 (0, 1, 4, 5, 8, 9)	=	(2, 3, 6, 7, 10, 11)
T_1I (0, 1, 4, 5, 8, 9)	=	(2, 3, 6, 7, 10, 11)
$T_{11}I$ (0, 1, 4, 5, 8, 9)	=	(0, 1, 4, 5, 8, 9)[28]

Elisabeth Lutyens

Thus all conditions are satisfied to produce an all-combinatorial hexachord. The trichord (0, 4, 8), combined with other non-self-mapping, even-numbered transpositions of itself, creates the whole-tone scale, which is also all-combinatorial.

Lutyens is extremely interested in symmetrical combinatorial shapes. In "Country of the Stars," she uses them in new, more disciplined, and more sophisticated ways than in the Wittgenstein motet. In the course of "Country of the Stars" she abandons twelve-note aggregates and uses three- and four-note combinations instead, which frees her to deal with alternative pitch structures. Her approach thus allows her freer use of tonal centers, trichords, and tetrachords without destroying the twelve-note structures.

Figure 2.4 illustrates how Lutyens uses the opening trichords as building blocks for larger aggregate structures. In this figure all combinations of (0, 1, 4), (0, 3 4), and (0, 4, 8) are listed, using the following procedure: any two n-chords can be added to produce twelve prime form aggregates using the formula $T_0(A) + T_n(B) =$ resultant chord C.

Figure 2.4. Prime form combinations of trichords (0, 1, 4), (0, 3, 4), and (0, 4, 8).

$T_0 + T$	$T_0 + T_0$	$T_0 + T_1$	$T_0 + T_2$	$T_0 + T_3$	$T_0 + T_4$	$T_0 + T_5$	$T_0 + T_6$	$T_0 + T_7$	$T_0 + T_8$	$T_0 + T_9$	$T_0 + T_{10}$	$T_0 + T_{11}$
0,1,4 +0,1,4	0,1,4	0,1,2,4,5	0,1,2,3,4,6	0,1,3,4,7	0,1,4,5,8	0,1,4,5,6,9	0,1,4,6,7,10	$+T_5$	$+T_4$	$+T_3$	$+T_2$	$+T_1$
0,1,4 + 0,3,4	0,1,3,4	0,1,4,5	0,1,2,4,5,6	0,1,3,4,6,7	0,1,4,7,8	0,1,4,5,8,9	0,1,3,4,7,9	0,1,2,3,6,9	0,3,4,5,8	0,3,4,7	0,2,3,4,6	0,1,2,3,4,5
0,1,4 + 0,4,8	0,1,4,8	0,1,4,5,8	0,2,3,4,6,8	0,1,2,4,5,8	T_0	T_1	T_2	T_3	T_0	T_1	T_2	T_3
0,4,8 + 0,4,8	0,4,8	0,1,4,5,8,9	0,2,4,6,8,10	0,1,4,5,8,9	T_0	T_1	T_2	T_1	T_0	T_1	T_2	T_1

Some combinations produce equivalent prime forms, thus limiting the number of possible resultant structures. Grouping the resultant possibilities into their n-chord class produces the following (Figure 2.5). Note the close resemblances between certain n-chords of different sizes: (0, 1, 4), (0, 1, 4, 5), (0, 1, 4, 5, 8).

Figure 2.5. Valid prime form combinations by n-chord.

Trichords	Tetrachords	Pentachords	Hexachords
0, 1, 4*	0, 1, 3, 4*	0, 1, 2, 4, 5	0, 1, 2, 3, 4, 6
0, 1, 8*	0, 1, 4, 5*	0, 1, 3, 4, 7*	0, 1, 4, 5, 6, 9
	0, 3, 4, 7*	0, 1, 4, 5, 8*	0, 1, 4, 6, 7, 10
	0, 1, 4, 8*	0, 1, 4, 7, 8	0, 1, 2, 4, 5, 6
		0, 3, 4, 5, 8	0, 1, 3, 4, 6, 7
		0, 2, 4, 6, 8	0, 1, 4, 5, 8, 9
			0, 1, 3, 4, 7, 9*
			0, 1, 2, 3, 6, 9
			0, 1, 2, 3, 4, 5
			0, 2, 3, 4, 6, 8
			0, 1, 2, 4, 5, 8*
			0, 3, 4, 5, 8, 9
			0, 2, 4, 6, 8, 10*

One of the techniques Lutyens uses is the combination of two or more n-chords. Successive applications can produce ever-larger sonority types. Often the inclusion of a given value to an n-chord produces a valid (n + 1)-chord. Figure 2.6 diagrams one particular path that Lutyens uses:

Figure 2.6. Lutyens' favored (n + 1) path in "Country of the Stars."

T_0 (0, 1,4)	=	(0, 1, 4)	=	"A"
A + T I (0, 1, 4)	=	(0, 1, 4, 5)	=	"B"
B + T^{11}(0, 1, 4)	=	(0, 1, 4, 5, 8)	=	"C"
C + T^4_7 I (0, 1, 4)	=	(0, 1, 4, 5, 8, 9)	=	"D"

Furthermore, the percentage of occurrences of the structures indicated in Figure 2.6 is shown in Figure 2.7, an approach called a "path technique."

Figure 2.7. The (0, 1, 4) + (0, 4, 8) path.

0, 1, 4 + 0, 4, 8	100%
0, 1, 4, 8	38.5%
0, 1, 4, 5, 8	81%
0, 1, 2, 4, 5, 8	40%

The n-chords in Figure 2.7 account for 69 percent of all the chords in "Country of the Stars." The overall percentage of prime form combinations (Figure 2.5) that Lutyens uses is approximately 90 percent.

There are deviant structures, however: n-chords that diverge from these prime forms. Although she resorts to them very infrequently, Lutyens may change the structure of an n-chord for a cadence or because of the text. Similarly, in the Wittgenstein *Motet*, Lutyens at times writes "wrong notes," pitches that cannot be explained as part of the work's hexachordal design. In "Country of the Stars," her distance from a valid prime n-chord form can be explained as another type of "wrong note" technique.[29] Lutyens never strays more than two moves away from any prime form except in $(0, 1, 2, 7)$, which is used twice as a passing chord and once at a strong cadence.

Another "wrong note" technique can be labeled "incompleteness." Several times Lutyens uses $(0, 1, 2, 5)$, a tetrachord two moves away from $(0, 1, 3, 4)$, one of the prime tetrachords, or an incomplete $(0, 1, 4, 5, 6, 9) = \{T_8(0, 1, 2, 5)\}$. Neither of these techniques is peculiar to Lutyens or to tonal composers of the past. Nonharmonic tones, upper and lower neighbor tones, and suspensions could be described as "wrong notes," and incomplete seventh chords or extra-tertian chords appear frequently in tonal music. In addition, Lutyens notes on the first page of the score that "the original title, some words and spelling have been changed [wrong notes] or simplified [incompleteness] in the interests of the singers or comprehensibility." Thus her treatment of the text parallels that of her musical materials.

Although Lutyens labels "Country of the Stars" a part-song (reviewers and critics call it a cantata), it is more like a motet. It demands the same careful attention to tuning that a sixteenth-century motet would take. John Alldis aptly wrote:

> Her feeling for words and the ideas they conjured up gave her choral works a romanticism which in spite of her classically refined textures appealed to the dramatic/communicative urge in the performers. The problem was to maintain her intellectual purpose against a glib, uncritical English ease.[30]

Lesser Works

De Amore (Op. 39) was written in June 1957, immediately following "Country of the Stars"; yet it did not receive its first performance until sixteen years later, in 1973. A cantata for soprano and tenor soloists, chorus, and moderately sized orchestra, the work was premiered at the Proms to favorable reviews. Lutyens chose portions of three poems by Chaucer: "The Parliament of Fowls," "The Prologue to the Legend of the Good Woman," and "Troilus and Creseide." *De Amore* depicts the delights and pleasures of love and nature and is direct in its expression and musical freshness.

In the early 1960s Edward Clark told Lutyens that she would never get the breakthrough she deserved while he was still alive; as it turned out, there was great truth in his statement, for he died in 1962, just when Lutyens began to come into her own.[31] At about the same time, William Glock was appointed controller of music at the BBC, a position he held until 1973. Under his leadership, BBC premiered eight new Lutyens works between 1960 and 1973, more than in any other comparable period.[32]

Quincunx is scored for unaccompanied baritone, wordless soprano, and orchestra. With this work, finished in 1960, the progressive paring down of materials and gestures that mark Lutyens' best music is firmly established. She describes her own compositional process at this time in connection with her Wind Quintet (1960):

> Shape and form remain my major preoccupations, before I even begin writing the piece, to ensure that the initial basic cell, however small, contains the possibilities within it for change and development in various proportions, tensions, relaxations, speeds, etc. in relation to each other. Once I have got my cell—probably but a few notes scribbled—the aural and formal possibilities grow in my mind: the why and wherefore, character and gesture of the whole work. Eventually I begin the writing down of the piece (alongside it any serial arrangement to be called upon).[33]

Lutyens wrote several choral works during the 1960s that deserve mention. In *Encomion*, for chorus, brass, and percussion, Lutyens sets her first scriptural text: Apocrypha (Sirach) 44:1-14, "Let Us Now Praise Famous Men." While she remembers that the piece got good performances in Liverpool, Lutyens most vividly recalls the program and poster announcing the concert: it was a Lutyens' work inside a Lutyens' work, for the piece was performed in the crypt of Liverpool's Metropolitan Cathedral, which her father had designed. *Hymn of Man* (1965), an extended, unaccompanied work for men's chorus (opus 61), was subsequently revoiced for SATB (opus 61a) in 1975. The text, a poem of the same name by Algernon Charles Swinburne, is a humanistic hymn of praise. Lutyens sets only twenty-two of the one hundred rhymed couplets of the original, not necessarily in Swinburne's order. Phrases of the music are dovetailed in rapid sequence to accommodate the wordy text, while other parts are spoken, whispered, and hummed. Throughout the work, tenors and basses are divided into eight parts, and divisi of up to fourteen parts occur. The total range for bass and tenor is extreme: B^{bl} to C ^{5}.[34] John Alldis, who commissioned the work, writes, "The tessitura was all wrong, either much too high or much too low, though she loved voices."[35]

For *Hymn of Man* Lutyens had chosen another philosophically intense poem, another intellectual puzzle. It is indeed not surprising that Lutyens places this humanistic parody of the biblical version of Creation among three choral works using biblical texts: *Encomion* and *Magnificat* and *Nunc Dimittis*. At no other time in any other kind of vocal music does she set sacred texts.[36] In these choral works of the 1960s Lutyens uses compositional techniques similar to those seen in *Motet* and "Country of the Stars."

Between the years 1963 and 1971 most of Lutyens' compositions resulted from commissions. Over 50 percent of these were works involving voices, and the texts were from increasingly varied sources. Encouraged by her contacts in the theater world, Lutyens again approached opera. Although composed without commission, her operas *The Numbered* and *Time Off—Not a Ghost of a Chance* were successful. Undoubtedly, *Time Off*, a charade in four scenes, is her best work for the stage. Although both include chorus, further discussion of these works lies outside the scope of this study.

The later 1960s brought not only more commissions and BBC performances but also other prestigious forms of recognition. In 1963 Lutyens received a cash award for composition from the Phoenix Trust; in 1969 the CBE (Commander of the British Empire) was bestowed on her by the Crown, and later that year she was awarded the City of London Midsummer Award for services to music. Lutyens' sixtieth year (1966) saw the first of a series of commemorative birthday concerts. (Others were given in 1971, 1976, and 1981.) Her fame spread through repeat broadcasts of her music over the BBC and concerts at Wigmore Hall, the Purcell Room, and the British Music Information Centre.

Although various publishers had initiated interest in Lutyens' prolific output (among them Mills Music Company, Schott, and Novello, who still hold copyrights to much of her music), she was never completely satisfied with the services she received from them. Having had years of professional experience as a copyist, she decided, in April of 1969, to found her own publishing house, Olivan. "Olivan Press," she later commented, "yielded more results in eighteen months than twenty-four years with four different and indifferent publishers."[37]

With awards, commemorative concerts, and her own press responding quickly to inquiries for her music, Lutyens began to get some long overdue recognition and was invited to lecture at colleges and universities. The inspiration for *Essence of Our Happinesses* (Op. 69), for chorus and orchestra, came from a question put to Lutyens by a young man at the Royal Academy of Music, who asked: Do you understand being interested only in music written now? Lutyens remembers "that 'now' immediately evoked for me the line from Donne: 'Before you sound that word, present, or that monosyllable, now, the present and the now is past.'"[38] The student's question led Lutyens to reread Donne's "Devotion XIV." At about the same time she received a book *Mysticism—Sacred and Profane*, by R. C. Zachner, based on experiences of timelessness and ecstasy achieved by such different means as mescaline and mysticism. She chose writings by Abu Yasid (a ninth-century Islamic mystic) and Rimbaud from among the many quoted in *Mysticism—Sacred and Profane*. Thus, *Essence of Our Happinesses*, whose title is taken from Donne's "Devotion," is built on texts by three poets from different periods, nationalities, and traditions.

The work opens with a short excerpt from a translation of Abu Yasid's "The Mi'raj of Abu Yasid," set for tenor and orchestra, followed by an instrumental dance movement, "Mystikos." The central piece, "Their Criticall Dayes," for tenor, chorus, and orchestra, is based on an abridged version of Donne's "Devotion XIV." "Chronikos," a second dance movement for orchestra, leads to a setting of lines by Rimbaud for tenor and orchestra. A final orchestra dance, "Manikos," ends the piece. The work is to be performed without breaks between movements.

The central movement of *Essence of Our Happinesses* is the spiritual core of the work. The opening uses four-part SATB choir; thereafter the choir alternates with the tenor soloist. Choral divisi reach as many as eleven parts in some short sections. Simple vertical sonorities are employed, but otherwise the texture is sparse. Unaccompanied recitative-like lines in individual vocal parts introduce the *tutti* sonorities. The work achieves a timeless effect through the subtlety of its musical events, the sparseness in the layout of melodic and harmonic incidents, and repetition of the musical material.

> All dynamism is banished, and we can almost feel the spacious air between statements. Again, where economy had in a sense been practised previously in her favorite palindromic forms, here the repetitions are no longer disguised by retrograde operations. Indeed the expressive point of the work is that we should be hypnotised by the thematic roundabout in which a recognisable train of objects continually revolves before us.[39]

Another choral work of this period is "Verses of Love" (1970), a part-song with divisions for unaccompanied mixed chorus with text by Ben Jonson. Economy of material, repetition, and variation immediately come to the fore in "Verses of Love." Although it looks deceptively short, this lovers' dialogue takes eight and a half minutes. Lutyens, always conscious of forms and compositional procedures of the past, uses "divisions" to signify variations, a characteristically English musical procedure in use during the mid-sixteenth and seventeenth centuries, Ben Jonson's time. Although Jonson's writing style is restrained and conservative, the dialogue is humorous and satiric. The words of the text generate the rhythmic flow of the piece.

"Verses of Love" contains three divisions, or dialogues, and no bar lines are indicated. In No. 1, "He of Her," the lover compares his sweetheart to beautiful natural images ("bright Lillie," "fall o' the Snow," "the bud o' the Briar"). The words in these verses belong to the lover (tenor voices). The sopranos, altos, and basses enter first, humming their parts, to prepare the way for the tenors' entrance, fanning out in half steps from a unison D^4 (Example 2.20).

Elisabeth Lutyens

Example 2.20. "Verses of Love," opening page.

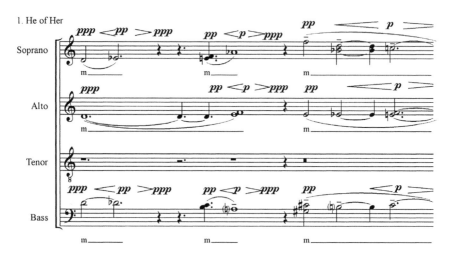

Between the tenor phrases, the fanning device recurs, alternating with the solo phrases for the rest of the movement. D acts as the center and gravitational force, drawing other pitches to it. While not strictly twelve-tone, this division uses compositional procedures drawn from serial techniques. The rhyme scheme of the text is

$a\ b\ a\ b\ c\ c^1\ a^1\ b^1\ a\ c^2$,

while the construction of the musical line that carries the text is

$a\ b\ a^1\ b^1\ c\ a\ b\ a^1\ b^1\ c$.

Lutyens' music accommodates the usual pattern in the rhyme scheme, which is also reflected subtly in her understanding of the variation form. The tenor line, bearer of the text, is delicate and unencumbered; nothing competes with it. In this division there is little tension and only a narrow dynamic range.

The contrasting personality of the woman comes through in the wider dynamic range and fluctuation of pitches introduced in the second division, "She of Him." Soprano and alto parts carry the text, sometimes together, sometimes alternating. Each melodic statement is a variation on the tenor line introduced in the first division. Inversion and augmentation are two devices seen on the opening page of movement II. The woman now enumerates the qualities she wants in her man. If there were such a person, she would be totally his. In this division the pitch center becomes $F^{\#}$, and a more consonant, sweet, third-related sound (2, 4, 6, 10) is apparent.

Greater dissonance returns in the third division, "His Last Word." Its opening is similar to that of the first division, but the man's last words are compressed— only two lines of text and music are needed: "I'le taste as lightly as the Bee, That doth but touch his flower, and flies away." When the man finds out that the woman will be his, he desires only an affair. Subtle variation of the melodic lines are apparent, the range is reduced, the intervals and rhythms are simplified, and choral voicings are varied from "He of Her."

Voice of Quiet Waters (1972) was commissioned by the BBC Northern Symphony Orchestra. Lutyens came across a phrase in Joseph Conrad's *Heart of Darkness*: "Between us there was . . . the bond of the sea." The idea of such a bond between Manchester and London became the basis of the work. Selecting prose from *Heart of Darkness*, William T. Palmer's *The River Mersey*, and a portion of a poem by William Wordsworth, Lutyens created a sixteen-minute work for orchestra and chorus. The first movement is a prelude. The chorus introduces a passage from *The River Mersey* that describes the various qualities of the river. After a brief orchestral interlude, the nocturne presents Conrad's description of the Thames. A second orchestral interlude follows, and then the final movement, "Chorale," a setting of Wordsworth's description of the river Duddon.

Counting Your Steps Op. 85 (1972), written for SATB chorus, four flutes, and four percussionists, was premiered by Michael Gielen and the members of the BBC orchestra and chorus.[40] The sound world of this piece differs from that of all the choral works previously discussed. Lutyens sets Central West African texts in translation, and her instrumentation, though not intended to be authentically African, captures the flavor of certain elements of African music.[41] The quartet of flutes includes bass flute, alto flute, and two normal-sized flutes doubling on piccolos. A large battery of percussion instruments is used: membranophones and idiophones in equal number.

For her texts Lutyens chose six poems from C. M. Bowra's *Primitive Song*.[42] The people of Central West Africa believe that each stage of life from birth to death must be celebrated in a fitting way. The human cycle—birth, growth, maturity, marriage, and death—is expressed freely in song. Lutyens' title, *Counting*

Your Steps, draws on a line used in the second movement, which expresses the feelings of a new bride as she leaves her home. Within the six short movements of the work, Lutyens conveys a life cycle.

I.   The tree have given its fruit (Ceremony of Birth/Spring)
II.   Counting, counting your steps (The Home-Leaving of the Bride)
III. On Sun, O Sun (Dance-Song)
IV.   My heart is all happy (Lullaby)
V.   And it is the great cold (Burial Chant)
VI.   And this is the end (Ghosts)

Lutyens' original ideas for the title are revealing: Birth to Burial, A Ceremony of Songs, Songs of the Human Cycle. The language of the poetry is simple: everyday experiences are told in a direct way, and nature images are used to convey the emotions of the singers and speakers. These texts are anonymous and speak of universal experiences. They are not abstract, dry, or theoretical, in stark contrast to the philosophical texts Lutyens chose for some of her earlier choral pieces.

While the rhyme schemes of the original poems may or may not be preserved in Bowra's translation, their repetition of words and phrases is clear and frequent. Often sequences and patterns of words appear, such as the series "animals, fish, birds, plants" in movements I and V. Lutyens uses simple binary, strophic, bar, and through-composed forms and, in the first movement, her own variation of a *forme fixe*. Three movements have subtitles: the third, "Dance-song," the fourth, "Lullaby," and the fifth, "Burial Chant."

Voices carry most of the weight of the work. Phrases are sung in unison or antiphonally, and less frequently, there are vertical sonorities. Much of the singing is divided between men and women. Men sing a phrase in unison; women respond. Movement II, "Counting, counting your steps (The Home-Leaving of the Bride)," is for women's voices in unison. Movement IV, "My heart is all happy," is for solo soprano and chorus women who whisper on indefinite pitches. The tenor soloist intones a chant in Movement V, "And it is the great cold." The men, and then the women, respond in unison. In Movement VI, "And this is the end," the women sing nonspecific pitches to the syllables "swiss" and "ping" for twenty-one measures, imitating the sounds of mosquitoes, while men speak the text; no definite pitches are indicated. Silence precedes the final, rhythmically notated, spoken gasp, *pianissimo*, "and this is the end."

Percussion instruments provide a constant underpinning for the flutes and voices, performing rhythmic ostinatos. An obvious example, in Movement II, is a drum pattern that permeates the texture, imitating the sound of footsteps as the bride leaves home. Atmospheric color is achieved by the variety of percussion instruments used: bongo drum, conga drums, metal gong drum, tom-toms, African drums, marimba, xylophone, claves, and whip, to name a few. In Movement VI, shells are rolled on the drum head while the male voices speak about the spirits of the dead. After a silence, the death rattle heard in the shake of the maracas concludes the work. The flutes, grouped mainly in homorhythmic patterns, accompany the voices or play introductory material in syncopated, jagged rhythms.

Most movements contain primitive elements. In the first movement, for example, there is a recurring pattern, sung in unison by the choir, to the syllables "yélè, yao, yao" (Example 2.21). In other movements, three- of four-note melodic ostinatos appear, as in Movement II, where the "counting your steps" motive is repeated six times in the voices while the same rhythm is reiterated in the bass flute, adding to the repeated footstep patterns in the percussion. In Movement III a short figure is repeated six times in sixteen measures: "death comes," "the tree falls," "the child is born," mm. 130-146.

Example 2.21. *Counting Your Steps*, mm. 30-36.

Lutyens works on two levels simultaneously in *Counting Your Steps*. Along-side the primitive elements, she employs more complex procedures of contemporary music. For example, in the opening measures of the work, the flutes introduce a series of tetrachords. The pitch content of the first movement, the work's longest and most involved, is generated from these block sonorities (Example 2.22).

Example 2.22. *Counting Your Steps*, mm. 1-8.

Although these twelve-note aggregates (composed of three tetrachords) recur throughout the movement, no row is apparent. One or more of the tetrachords generated here appears in subsequent movements. Not until the last movement is an unencumbered row revealed, the row that generated the aggregate structures of the opening measures (Example 2.23).

Example 2.23. *Counting Your Steps*, mm. 245-250.

Although elements of this row can be discerned in Movements I, II, and III, one is never sure until the final movement what the exact pitch sequence and content of the row is. Movement IV, a simple lullaby, uses some of the above-mentioned tetrachords, and its melody utilizes a very small range, except for an octave displacement in the line. In Movement V, the Burial Chant, only five tones are used in the vocal lines—even less pitch content. In this movement "the prisoner is free." Toward the end, one realizes how one fits into life, into the chain of events, "animal, bird, fish, man."

In *Counting Your Steps*, Lutyens uses frequent repetition and simply patterned ideas. Here, more than elsewhere, atmospheric writing and primitive and contemporary techniques coexist. Compared to her earlier works, *Counting Your Steps* uses less complex harmony, simpler gestures, reduced eventfulness; powerful silences obscure, then reveal the modern techniques that provide the connective tissue and formal logic of the whole work.

Lutyens completed two other choral works before her death in April 1983: "It Is the Hour" Op. 111a (1976), for unaccompanied mixed chorus and with a text by Byron, and "Roots of the World" Op. 136 (1979), which has a text by W. B. Yeats and is scored for mixed chorus and cello obbligato.

Lutyens has always had a loyal following, and during the last decade of her life her closest friends were avant garde musicians younger than she. These were the people who appreciated her music, her uncompromising spirit and fearlessness, and her commitment to new music. Robert Saxton writes:

> Lutyens shines out as one of the few composers who have maintained a burning vision—both musically and extra-musically—which, even when not perfectly achieved, defines a path which is individual, of markedly strong character, and which outlines a poetic strength of piercing beauty.[43]

The last word must go to Lutyens. In a talk called "All Our Tomorrows," she remarked:

> We are too often labeled at our musical birth and sent on our various journeys according to the ticket allotted us. Artists are now denominated more by their "styles" than their individual voices. "Op" forever is a fearful thought; "Dodecaphonic" for decades a dull vista. I know I personally suffered from the label 12-tone hung around my neck in the thirties that was meant to send me to swift oblivion. I may not yet know my final musical destination—but it shall be one of my own choice not that of an issuer of tickets and labels.[44]

Notes

1. Elisabeth Lutyens, *A Goldfish Bowl* (London: Cassell and Co., 1972), 9.

2. Elisabeth Lutyens, "Mothers and Daughters," TV interview series done for British television, 1981. In this poignant and revealing interview, Lutyens vividly remembers her childhood with lines such as, "My mother gave me my first feeling of unrequited love."

3. Harold Darke studied composition with Stanford at the Royal College of Music and stayed on to teach there from 1919 to 1969. He was organist at St. Michael's from 1919 to 1966, where he founded the St. Michael's Singers. He composed extensively for organ and choir. Lutyens might have been placed with Ralph Vaughan Williams or John Ireland, composers who, in retrospect, she relegated to the "cow-pat school of composition" (unpublished article, July 2, 1971).

4. Iris Lemare, quoted in Ernest Chapman, "The Macnaghten Concerts," *Composer* 57 (Spring 1976): 14.

5. Francis Routh, *Contemporary British Music—The Twenty-Five Years from 1945-1970* (London: Macdonald and Co., 1971), 319.

6. Since Lutyens' book was written in 1972, Clark has received some overdue recognition, especially in Nicholas Kenyon's *BBC Symphony Orchestra* (London: BBC, 1981).

7. Kenyon, *BBC Symphony Orchestra.*

8. Lutyens, *A Goldfish Bowl,* 139.

9. *The New Grove Dictionary of Music and Musicians,* s.v. "Elisabeth Lutyens," by Anthony Paine.

10. Humphrey Searle and Robert Layton, *Britain, Scandanavia and The Netherlands,* Twentieth Century Composers, vol. 3 (London: Wiedenfeld and Nicolson, 1972), 91.

11. Three works, all dealing with the idea of victim, share a musical theme: *The Pit, Requiem for the Living,* and the ballet *Rhadamantus.* The notion, Lutyens writes in an unpublished preface to the three works, had its origins in the friend-

ship of someone who preferred failure and grievance to achievement and success (a death-wisher).

12. GNS, "The Viola as Prima Donna and Other Improbabilities," *Music Review* 11 (1950): 322.

13. *The New Grove Dictionary of Music and Musicians*, s.v. "Elisabeth Lutyens," by Anthony Paine.

14. See Appendix A for more information on the Composer's Concourse.

15. See Appendix B for a complete, chronological listing of Lutyens' choral output from the catalog of available works.

16. See Appendix C for a complete listing of all withdrawn works that are in the British Museum.

17. See Appendix D for the complete text of *Requiem for the Living*.

18. See Appendix E for the complete text of the *Motet*.

19. In mathematics, "mapping" is a transformation taking the points of one space into the points of the same or another space.

20. The analytical approach to the serial procedures discussed in this chapter is taken from John Rahn, *Basic Atonal Theory* (New York: Longman, 1975).

21. (C, C#, E) and (C, E^b, E) exhibit a symmetrical relationship: (0, 1, 4) : : (0, -1, -4).

22. Consider that any two groups of integers are identical if they can be made equal by adding or subtracting a constant from one group. Thus C, E^b, E = (0, 3, 4) and F, A^b, A = (5, 8, 9); therefore:

$$\begin{array}{r} 5\ \ 8\ \ 9 \\ -\ \ 5\ \ 5\ \ 5 \\ \hline 0\ \ 3\ \ 4 \end{array}$$

If any two units have this relationship, then we can say that the pair is congruent. Sonority will therefore be labeled by the smallest congruent integer set that can be applied to it. Thus the (5, 8, 9) sonority will fall into the (0, 3, 4) category.

23. N.B. The case can be made that because of the combinatorial nature of the hexachords, any two linear voices would exhibit palindromic structures if one would transpose or invert one of the voices. I am only including in this discussion those combinatorial hexachords that are explicitly stated, without transposition or inversion, as, for example, mm. 25-30.

24. Anthony Milner, quoted in Howard Hartog, ed., *European Music in the Twentieth Century* (New York: Praeger, 1957), 145.

25. John Alldis, "Modern Choral Music," *Composer* 33 (Autumn 1969): 11.

26. Both in Lutyens' catalogue and in the British Museum collection of Lutyens holdings, "Country of the Stars" is dated 1963, confusing the date of the first performance with the date of composition. The work was commissioned by *The Musical Times* and is printed in the August 1963 issue, with several critiques of the first performance. The same article includes a list of Lutyens' works and lists

"Country" under 1956. The most recent listing, compiled in *New Music 1988* by Glyn Perrin (the executor of the Lutyens estate), dates "Country" 1957/1963.

27. For example, a D major triad is outlined in m. 28.

28. T stands for transposition

T_0 maps to itself

T_2 maps to its complement

T_1I maps to its complement

$T_{11}I$ maps to itself

29. "Distance" refers to the shortest number of moves a given n-chord must make before it becomes a valid n-chord (generated from two or more prime trichords). "Move" is defined as the transposition of one element by one value. Thus (0, 1, 3) to (0, 1, 4) is one move, (0, 1, 3) to (0, 1, 6) is three moves, and (0, 1, 3) to (0, 2, 4) is two moves.

30. Letter from John Alldis to Catherine Roma, October 10, 1987.

31. Edward Clark felt that his position as champion of the new music (the Second Viennese School in particular) and his strong opinions about English provincialism hampered Lutyens' career. Critics Martin Quinlan and John Davenport comment on Clark: "Never an organization man, he resigned (after some furious row) to become, so far as the BBC was concerned, an 'unperson.'" Martin Quinlan, *The London Times*, February 22, 1973, 10. "His taste was as fastidious as it was catholic, and his contempt for the pretentious and the imbecile was sometimes expressed with a startling force that annihilated the philistine and delighted his innumerable friends all over Europe and America." John Davenport, "Mr. Edward Clark," *The London Times*, May 8, 1962, 16.

32. In 1948 William Glock founded the Summer School at Bryanston, Dorset, which in 1953 moved to Dartington Hall, Devon. The first of many pieces he commissioned from Lutyens was *Motet*, and Dartington saw its first performance.

33. *A Goldfish Bowl*, 267-268.

34. Octave identification based on American Physical and Acoustical Society System.

35. Letter from John Alldis to Catherine Roma, October 10, 1987.

36. *Magnificat* and *Nunc Dimittis* (1965) were written for the choir at Coventry Cathedral.

37. *A Goldfish Bowl*, 301.

38. Elisabeth Lutyens, from a program note written for the first performance of *Essence* by the BBC on September 8, 1970.

39. Anthony Payne, "Elisabeth Lutyens's *Essence of Our Happinesses*," *Tempo* 95 (1970): 33.

40. There is a discrepancy between opus numbers and dates for *Voice of Quiet Waters*, listed as Op. 84, completed in London, April 11, 1972, and *Counting Your Steps*, listed as Op. 85, completed in January 1972. The first performance of *Voice* took place on April 14, 1972, and *Counting* was premiered on May 22, 1972.

41. Some of the African idioms Lutyens uses in *Counting Your Steps* are unison singing, responsorial style, vocables that imitate nature's sounds, and simple musical forms.

42. Lutyens makes the following acknowledgments at the end of her score: Poems by the Gabon Pygmies (*Les Pygmees de la Foret Equitoriale* and *L'Ame du Pygmee d'Afrique*, R. P. Trilles) from *Primitive Song* by C. M. Bowra (Cleveland: World Publishing Co., 1962).

43. Robert Saxton, "Elisabeth Lutyens," *Yearbook 1988* (London: Oxford University Press), 16.

44. Elisabeth Lutyens, "All Our Tomorrows," unpublished article, n.d.

Elizabeth Maconchy (1907-1994)

Elizabeth Maconchy was born in Broxbourne, Hertford, north of London, on March 19, 1907. Although both parents were Irish, her family lived in Buckinghamshire for several years before moving to Dublin after World War I. Elizabeth began piano lessons at an early age, and comments: "I started writing when I was six. It came completely out of the blue. We moved to Ireland when I was quite small; my family being unmusical, I didn't hear any music at all except what I could play myself."[1] Lifelong friend and colleague Anne Macnaghten amplifies Maconchy's remarks.

> There was very little in the background of Elizabeth Maconchy to account for her musical genius. Her father played the piano a little, and her mother was quite unmusical. Of her two sisters, one was tone deaf and the other only mildly interested. . . . Her first experience of a concert was hearing the Hallé in Dublin when she was fifteen. But at age six she began, unprompted, to write pieces for the piano.[2]

Maconchy's father died when she was fifteen, and in the following year her mother brought the children back to England. That same year, 1923, at the age of sixteen, Elizabeth was accepted into the Royal College of Music: "Coming to London as a music student was a plunge into life, and once I had found my feet I enjoyed my time at the RCM immensely."[3] She studied piano with Arthur Alexander, counterpoint with C. H. Kitson, and composition with Charles Wood and Ralph Vaughan Williams. She worked with Vaughan Williams for many years, and acknowledges:

> Studying with Vaughan Williams helped me tremendously; everything suddenly opened out to me: it was a whole new world when I became a pupil of his, not so much from his teaching as just from him as a person, his attitude to music. He was a tremendously inspiring person.[4]

Vaughan Williams encouraged his students to learn by trial and error, much as he had done. He mistrusted brilliance, and he believed in finding things out by doing. During her first year of study with him, Maconchy discovered the music of Bela Bartók, which at that time was not well known in London: "I think Vaughan Williams' and Bartók's influence had much the most effect on me during those formative years, and I don't think later influences counted nearly so much."[5]

From Vaughan Williams she learned the importance of having new works performed for colleagues in order to gain constructive criticism. Vaughan Williams and Gustav Holst regularly met to exchange critiques of one another's music. To this end, Maconchy and her student-colleagues Grace Williams and Imogen Holst met and performed their emerging compositions for one another.

During her six years at the Royal College of Music, Maconchy won the Blumenthal and Sullivan Scholarships. In 1929 she was awarded the Octavia Traveling Scholarship and visited Vienna and Paris. At the recommendation of a teacher at the RCM, she spent two months in Prague studying with Karel Jirák.[6] Her music aroused much interest, and she returned to Prague in 1930 when her piano concerto was premiered by Schulhoff and the Prague Philharmonic. Maconchy would later travel to Prague (1935), Cracow, and Warsaw (1939) for performances of her works by the International Society for Contemporary Music (ISCM).

> When I returned from Prague I did the only thing then open to a young composer—sent a score to Sir Henry Wood. I was fortunate—and he played my suite *The Land* at the Proms the same season. It received, though I say it, staggeringly good press notices—but that was all. No one gave me a commission, or a grant, or a chatty interview, or another performance.[7]

The same week of the Proms performance, Maconchy married William LeFanu, a member of a well-known Irish literary family. *The Land* was a work that especially excited Holst, and after its premiere at the Proms, he was overheard saying to LeFanu, "Keep her at it." Donald Francis Tovey, too, in a note of appreciation, wrote: "Miss Maconchy, like Beethoven, achieves *Ausdruck der Empfindung* (expression of emotion)."[8]

From these early works it is apparent that Maconchy had her own distinctive voice and was receiving favorable press notices and recognition from people in important places.[9] She had never felt prejudice toward the performance of student compositions at the RCM, nor had she felt any discrimination because she was a woman. However, once out of the academy, Maconchy discovered there would be no performances of her works unless she sought them.

Her early career did not flourish as one might have expected after this brilliant start. Constant Lambert said, "There are regrettably few young composers of any particular talent today, but in Benjamin Britten and Elizabeth Maconchy we have two whose future development should be of great interest."[10] However, unlike Britten, Tippett, Walton, and Lutyens (the other leading woman of her generation), Maconchy remained a very private person, with a strong yet quiet nature. Perhaps this is explained by Maconchy's hard-fought struggle with tuberculosis. In 1932 she became ill but refused to go to Switzerland and instead moved to Brighton, outside of London. The severity of the tuberculosis did put Maconchy out of the musical mainstream for a time, and this was, in one sense, a restricting factor. However, in her solitude, she was able to develop her own line of thought and individuality, and she never stopped writing. Maconchy focused on chamber music, concentrating specifically on the string quartet, which forms the core of her output.

In the early 1930s three young women, led by Elisabeth Lutyens (a friend and colleague of Maconchy's at the RCM),[11] were facing the same difficulties as Maconchy in receiving performances of their works. Lutyens put Anne Macnaghten in touch with Maconchy, and the Macnaghten Quartet premiered Maconchy's first string quartet at the Macnaghten-Lemare Concerts in 1933. The same year the BBC performed her oboe quintet, which later won the *Daily Telegraph* Competition. Toward the end of the decade Maconchy composed two more quartets, and in 1937 her second quartet was performed for the ISCM in Paris. Three orchestral works won first performances by the BBC. Donald Tovey invited her to Edinburgh for performances of her music, and Sir Henry Wood introduced additional works at the Proms.

Maconchy became intrigued with serial technique and experimented with it in the early 1940s. She did not choose to use it then and has not since, commenting:

> I gave myself a course of twelve-tone technique during the War for interest and I decided it wasn't the way I wanted to write my music. . . . I was already an economical composer. I found it thematically inhibiting rather than a liberating technique. Though where tonality or atonality is concerned, it has helped me to greater freedom.[12]

The war curtailed performances of her works in London but did not keep Maconchy from composing several more string quartets. The demands of motherhood were great both before and after the war. Two daughters were born to Elizabeth and William: Anne in 1939 and Nicola in 1947. In spite of these circumstances, Maconchy continued to gain more recognition. One of her works was performed in Copenhagen for the ISCM (1947), and her fifth string quartet won the Edwin Evans Prize. In 1953, the coronation year, she won the London County Council Prize for her orchestral work *The Thames*. At this time she also began her long association with the Composer's Guild.[13] By 1955, the BBC had scheduled a concert of all six quartets on a program featuring contemporary composers.

In the fifty-year period from 1933 to 1984 Elizabeth Maconchy wrote thirteen string quartets. She is the English composer most closely associated with this medium.[14]

> Writing chamber music has been my own main preoccupation. I have found the string quartet above all best suited to the expression of the kind of music I want to

write—music as an impassioned argument. And in this medium I have worked mainly with contrapuntal ideas—that is, a counterpoint of rhythm as well as melodic lines.[15]

Certain parallels can be drawn between Maconchy's string quartets and the six of Bela Bartók. Both reveal highly contrapuntal textures, short chromatic motives, and canonic procedures. However, Maconchy's music is not derived from folk music as is that of Bartók, Vaughan Williams, or Janáček—composers with whom she is constantly compared. Although these people were powerful influences, she adopted a more abstract musical process and ignored the folk influence. It is in the string quartet that Maconchy works through her musical development. Although she does not play a stringed instrument, she feels most at home writing for strings. For Maconchy, the string quartet is the perfect vehicle for dramatic expression, as if four characters were engaged in statement and comment.

> Dramatic and emotional tension is created by means of counterpoint in much the same way as happens in a play. The characters are established as individuals, each with his own differentiated characteristics: the drama then grows from the interplay of these characters—the clash of their ideas and the way in which they react upon each other.[16]

Upon completion of her seventh string quartet (1956), Maconchy experienced a creative block. In her own words, "I felt stuck. I was tired of using the same forms, and I needed to break away from chamber music in general."[17] She began to write operas and found it immensely stimulating—an endeavor that led her into new compositional forms. The three one-act operas—*The Sofa* (1956-1957), *The Three Strangers* (1958-1967), and *The Departure* (1960-1961)—were written within a ten-year period to the virtual exclusion of chamber music composition. In the church opera, *The Jesse Tree* (1970), Maconchy and librettist Anne Ridler took the Jesse Tree window in Dorchester Abbey and various old myths as their inspiration. All of these chamber operas include chorus.

Also during this time, Maconchy contributed several practical works for children's voices: operas, extravaganzas, scenas, and musical theater works. *The Birds* (1967-1968), commissioned by Bishop's Shortford College, combines strong, uninhibited choruses to represent the collective birds, with one or two solos that do not tax young voices too much. Maconchy wrote her own libretto, based on Aristophanes' play by the same title; there are several interpolated, spoken episodes, some of topical significance, which may be devised by the local performing group. Other works for children's voices include: *Samson and the Gates of Gaza* (1963-1964), *Johnny and the Mohawks* (1969), *Fly-By-Nights* (1973), and *The King of the Golden River* (1974-1975). Hugo Cole remarks:

> Maconchy has continued to advance into new country. . . . She has also learnt how to put her full creative strength into works for children and amateurs while still writing in a simple and approachable way. *The Birds* has something of the

gusto and good humour of Vaughan Williams's more popular works for amateurs; *Samson* and *The King of the Golden River* are strongly dramatic and individual, yet never overstep the limits of what is practicable for children.[18]

Accompanying her interest and enthusiasm for opera and setting text came a rich outpouring of choral music. From 1962 to 1987, Maconchy contributed twenty-five works to the choral repertoire, most of them on commissions. Although her concept of "impassioned argument" may not translate perfectly from strings to voices, Maconchy uses similar compositional techniques in the choral works as in the string quartets. The overall texture is contrapuntal, although in the choral works it is a counterpoint of textures and colors more than it is a "counterpoint of rhythm as well as melodic lines."[19] Short, generative cells, introduced early in the work, are the building materials of her varied textures, and Maconchy uses them skillfully and economically. Homophonic writing appears with equal effectiveness.

Maconchy's harmonic language is tonal, with well-defined pitch centers. She uses scalar material other than major and minor, and she occasionally will move into ambiguous tonal areas for text-painting purposes. She also incorporates a high degree of chromatic color. Individual lines can produce dissonances; often the vertical dissonance occurs as a byproduct of her linear approach.

Melodic lines are lyrical, and Maconchy achieves balance in the range and tessitura of individual vocal lines. The more challenging musical passages are never carried out at the expense of idiomatic handling of the voice. Individual vocal lines are well defined, sometimes disjunct, but not too difficult to sing.

Maconchy has a gift for selecting appropriate texts for her vocal and choral works. She believes that the greatest poetry is simply great in itself; some texts ask to be set to music, while there is no harm in setting others.[20] Personal involvement with the words is paramount for Maconchy. The words must always have an exact relationship to the music, and music cannot go away from them.[21] Maconchy's sensitivity to setting text can be seen in the natural way in which her rhythms develop. Frequent changes of meter and subdivision of the beat occur whenever necessary to accommodate the text in a fresh, meaningful way. She has set texts primarily by English poets, from whom she has derived great inspiration: John Donne, Dylan Thomas, Sir Walter Raleigh, Dame Edith Sitwell, William Blake, Percy Bysshe Shelley, and especially Gerard Manley Hopkins. However, she preferred anonymous medieval texts for her Christmas anthems.

Maconchy wrote only two sets of choral compositions prior to 1962.[22] Her first, *Two Motets* (1932), is based on "A Hymn to Christ" and "A Hymn to God the Father," poems by John Donne. Reflecting the serious nature of these texts, Maconchy employs thick textures and dark colors. The motets are scored for unaccompanied double chorus and intended for a large ensemble. *Six Yeats Settings* (1951) represents her only use of texts by someone from her native country. The work is based on six short, deceptively simple poems by Yeats about youth's folly, rigors, and traps of love, and the wisdom of age. Unlike *Two Motets*, the texture of the Yeats set is thinner and more transparent. The set is scored for women's chorus, clarinet, harp, and two optional horns.[23]

Maconchy's choral works during the last quarter century can be divided into pieces for unaccompanied chorus, works for chorus and chamber-sized ensemble, and pieces for chorus and orchestra. The largest category encompasses fifteen pieces for unaccompanied chorus. Seven of these works are short, accessible Christmas settings, using traditional medieval texts, such as "I Sing of a Maiden" (1966) and "There Is No Rose" (1985). Two of the seven Christmas settings are for unchanged voices; the remaining five are for mixed chorus.

The unaccompanied, nonseasonal works include a variety of texts. "Propheta Mendax" (The Lying Prophet), medieval in origin, is a moral vignette about theft and false prophets, and was commissioned and performed by the Vienna Boys' Choir in 1966. A very dramatic, graphic text by Louis MacNeice, "Prayer before Birth" (1971), is set for a four-part women's chorus. "Two Epitaphs" (1975) are miniature part-songs for SSA, which use texts from gravestones in Dorchester Abbey. *Nocturnal* (1965), "Siren's Song" (1971), and *Creatures* (1979) receive frequent performances and will be examined in more detail.

Among Maconchy's more recent additions to the choral repertoire are two popular collections of short pieces: *Four Miniatures* (1979) and *Creatures. Still Falls the Rain* (1985), for double choir, was Maconchy's last substantial choral work. The poem "Still Falls the Rain" by Dame Edith Sitwell is rich in images and complex poetic techniques. Maconchy's already thick texture is enriched with the addition of four solo soprano lines. Like several of the poems Maconchy chooses to set, despair is followed by hope, darkness by light, dissonance by consonance.

Nocturnal

Nocturnal, written for the 1965 Cork International Festival, was Maconchy's first unaccompanied choral work since *Two Hymns* (1932). It is a continuous setting of poems by three different authors: William Barnes (1801-1886), Edward Thomas (1878-1917), and Percy Bysshe Shelley (1792-1822). Maconchy explains:

> The phrase "will you come?" links the first poem by William Barnes to the second by Edward Thomas; in the Shelley poem it becomes "come soon." The approach of night, which gives all three poems their nocturnal feeling, is gradual: evening begins to approach at the end of the Barnes poem; the Edward Thomas is a real twilight poem, with flashes of sights and sounds half-seen and heard; and then night slowly falls in the Shelley poem. I have treated these three poems like the panels of a triptych—three contracted pieces which are at the same time linked by idea and by technical means.[24]

While *Nocturnal* is an ode to night, the separate poems do not necessarily refer to the approach of night. The juxtaposition of poems leads the listener to new levels of meaning. The first two poems are apostrophes in which a lover romantically implores, "Will you come?" The appeal is most likely to a maiden or to the dark, mysterious night personified as a woman. The lover asks, in the first poem, if she will come in early spring or fall. He asks whether she will come when Whitsuntide brings longer days, but the second poem makes clear that he really means to ask if she will respond anytime—at noon, at night, by the full moon, or in morning. The imploring of the lover himself and the repetition of "will you come?" underscores the sense of urgency.

In the third poem, night may be seen as peace or oblivion or the beloved personified.[25] The earlier texts take on new meaning in juxtaposition with the third, a meaning not intended by the other authors, and in retrospect, one hears the first and second poems differently. Perhaps the linked poems are a metaphor for the passing of time or for fleeting youth, or constitute an appeal to night to come and surround the listener with the awareness of how fleeting time is.

Maconchy's clever choice and combination of texts poses a rhetorical question, repeated throughout the triptych. With ingenuity and imagination she has created a new dimension by juxtaposing and combining three unrelated poems. The numerous repeated phrases keep the important questions of the text ever-present. At the end, the question is left unanswered, the situation ambivalent. Interpretation is left to the listener.

Nocturnal is one of Maconchy's most economical pieces. The compositional material for the three connected movements grows out of a single melodic gesture found in the soprano in measure 1 (Example 3.1).

Example 3.1. *Nocturnal*, mm. 1-2.

The gesture consists of six different pitches with F# as the pitch center, and can be divided into two cells, A and B (see Example 3.1). Maconchy places a dotted line after the first four pitches, which serves to delineate the cells. It also demonstrates a rhythmic organization based on eighth-note motion rather than the common quarter-note tactus. In this context, the eighth notes are divided into a pattern of five plus three, moving toward the note of resolution. This organization provides an inherent lyricism to the opening melodic gesture.

Cell A consists of a whole step and a fourth, implying a pentatonic sound. The introduction of the pitches A and E in cell B throws a different light and color onto the phrase. E and A weaken the pentatonic sound of the previous cell, but do not weaken F# as the tonal center. The opening cell is heard as consonant; the second cell adds the dissonance. This musical relationship of consonance versus dissonance, set up in the first measure of *Nocturnal*, operates throughout the rest of the work.

Maconchy introduces a supporting harmony in m. 2 in the male voices that acts as a tonic sonority for the entire piece (Example 3.2). It recurs as a recognizable pillar after more dissonant pantonal sections.

Example 3.2. *Nocturnal*, mm. 1-3.

The sonority consists of a trichord based on F# (m. 2, beat 3) and reinforces the F# tonal center already established in the soprano. Preceding this trichord is another sonority based on G , which functions as a neighbor chord to the F# trichord. This relationship is heard in a variety of ways, always in the lower voices, and is developed in a number of places in the piece. The relationship of these two sonorities is again one of dissonance to consonance.

The relationship between these trichords is expanded and used on a larger plane in the piece. A frequently used variation of the neighbor chord sonority is found in m. 11 in the male voices. When the pitch center shifts, either C#4 or C#3 are in the bass, with G and B in the tenor voices. This same sonority returns in the opening and closing measures of Movement II and in the final measures of Movement III (enharmonically spelled). Another example of the play between neighbor chord and tonic sonority is found within Movement II (Example 3.3).

Example 3.3. *Nocturnal*, mm. 56-61.

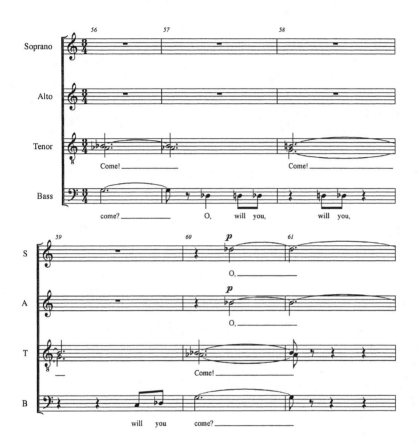

Cells A and B are used in a variety of ways. In Movement I, the bass entrance in m. 2 is initially based on cell A (see Example 3.2). The range has been decreased from a fourth to a major third, but the overall rhythm has been preserved. In m. 3, the second part of the phrase has been chromatically embellished with the addition of F natural. The sonorities in the tenor and bass voices (mm. 2-3) move from consonance to dissonance. This particular alteration is used in subsequent movements.

In m. 12 the bass voices introduce cell A in the dominant spelled as D^b. The sopranos enter in m. 13 and create a stretto with the basses. Up to now, the variations of the cells have been introduced subtly and fleetingly. In mm. 15-20, Maconchy expands her harmonic palette, her use of dissonance through chromatic alteration becomes more overt, and the tonal center becomes increasingly ambiguous. While the melodic lines in this passage may approach whole tone scales, occasional half-steps complicate the harmonic structure. The text sets up the change in harmonic idiom: the passage is starkly dissonant when the word "love" appears for the first time (Example 3.4).

Example 3.4. *Nocturnal*, mm. 15-20.

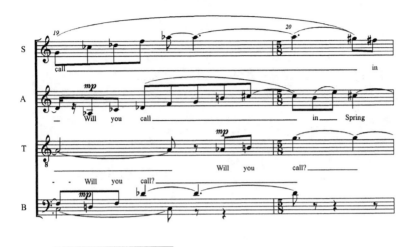

In m. 23, cell A returns in the soprano (with octave displacement on F#), and the bass variation reappears exactly as in m. 2. The first movement, not unlike a movement in basic ternary form (ABA), presents the principal motives, cells A and B, mm. 1-6; the first theme is restated in the dominant, mm. 13-14. In the middle section, the most blistering dissonance occurs, tonal ambivalence takes over, all for text purposes. The restatement occurs in m. 23, and no new material is introduced to the end of the movement.

Movement II is the most dissonant of the three. The tonal center is ambiguous from the start, yet each cell is recognizable and related to the opening measures of Movement I. Bartók's influence on Maconchy can be seen in her frequent use of the gapped scale[26] (Example 3.5), a scale created from the chromatic adjustment of cell A, seen in m. 3 of the first movement in the bass part.

Example 3.5. *Nocturnal*, mm. 79-82.

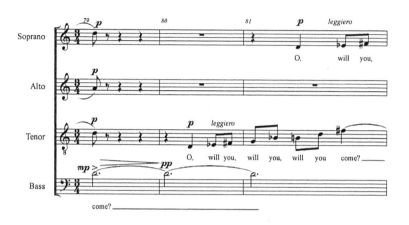

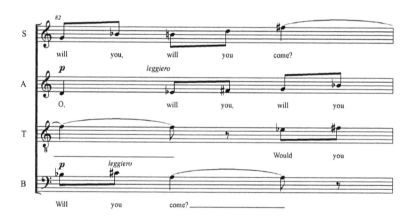

Movement III begins in a low, rich register. The time is later in the night, and this is the warmest moment in the work. Perhaps it is not ironic that the opening of this third movement should be so inviting, so solid and sonorous. Shelley wants to be touched by night's magic wand; he yearns for the night—not death, not sleep, but the dark, inviting night—to surround him. The basses reintroduce a pedal on G♭2 (heard as F#), the lowest use of pitch in the piece (Example 3.6). The baritones present a rocking 6-5 motion above the G♭. The tenors then enter in m. 133 with the same rocking 6-5 motion, slightly out of phase with the baritones. A chromatic

embellishment of this figure follows in m. 133. The 6-5 motion is a double consonance, and with the addition of the chromatic embellishment the consonance and
dissonance relationship is maintained.

Example 3.6. *Nocturnal*, mm. 131-132.

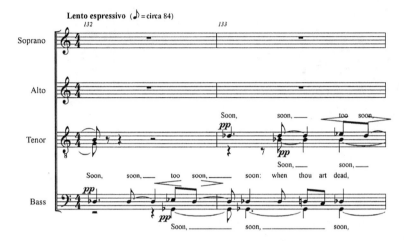

The immediately recognizable cell A returns in m. 145, with the text "Will you
come?" It is accompanied by a tonicized sonority based on C#, the dominant of F#.
The piece ends paradoxically, asking the unanswerable question and leaving it
unresolved. The glissando in the last measure ascends *morendo, a niente* (Example 3.7).

Example 3.7. *Nocturnal*, mm. 147-149.

Bartók's influence on Maconchy is noticeable in her use of the single melodic gesture, reduced to two cells, which are generative of the whole work. Her
use of nontraditional, synthetic scales and pitch tonality, and her commanding use
and understanding of consonance versus dissonance are reminiscent of Bartók. In
Nocturnal, Maconchy, like Bartók, has created her own style of night music, which
can be heard in works such as his fourth string quartet, the third piano concerto, or
the *Music for Strings, Percussion, and Celesta*. Maconchy's night music is more
lyrical and impressionistic.

"Siren's Song"

"Siren's Song" was commissioned by the Louis Halsey Singers and is scored for
SSATB chorus with soprano and tenor soloists. Maconchy selected several couplets from the opening pages of *The Inner Temple Masque*[27] by William Browne
(1591-1643), a Jacobean poet who wrote in the style of Spenser. The masque con-
cerns the mythological characters Ulysses and Circe, and Browne opens the drama
with a scene depicting the sirens.[28] In Greek mythology, the sirens were the virgin
daughters of the sea-god Phorcys. Their enchanting voices and sweet song were so
beautiful that sailors were lured to shipwreck and death as they traveled past the
siren's rocky coastline. In "Siren's Song" the women represent the sirens, and the
men represent the sailors. In the score, Maconchy specifies that the sopranos and
altos should be placed at a little distance from the tenors and basses.

The piece begins with a textless call by the sirens, singing cascading sighs
based on the whole tone scale. The women's voices, in three-part divisi, begin
pianissimo, poco lento, liberamente. These opening measures sound tonal, yet
Maconchy introduces chromatic pitches that produce more complicated sonorities

without completely losing the whole tone sound. These descending scalar motives return throughout the work (Example 3.8).

Example 3.8. "Siren's Song," mm. 1-4.

Maconchy uses a recurring trichord, first introduced in m. 11 by the soprano voices. This sonority, based on whole tones, is preceded by a double appoggiatura that quickly resolves as the sirens guide the sailors to shore, "steer, hither steer." The trichord, with appoggiatura, appears every time the word "steer" is sung. Notice the resemblance to Debussy's *Sirènes* (Example 3.9).

Example 3.9. "Siren's Song," mm. 11-14.

Hearing the sirens' call for them, and echoing in response, the men's voices enter for the first time in m. 13. The tenors and basses are an amplification of the original call, and they are divided in the same manner as the women's voices.

In m. 16, the sopranos and altos complete the phrase "steer hither your wingéd pines." Chorus women always take the lead, initiating the enticing text. The only exception is at the end, and for good reason. Maconchy adds two words not in the original text, "we come," which the men sing in the final measure of the work. At this point the listener knows the sirens have succeeded in seducing the sailors. It is also the point in the piece where all the motives and melodic materials appear simultaneously. While first sopranos sing the final line of text, the second sopranos sing a variation of the "steer" trichord, and the altos sing the opening "ahs." The tenors present the "ah" motive for the first time, and the basses sing a descending motive, which rocks gently up and down (Example 3.10). All voices glissando to a unison E^{b4} in m. 57. The unison is symbolic of the union: the sailors meet their fate, as they are dashed upon the rocks following the sirens' song.

Example 3.10. "Siren's Song," mm. 52-57.

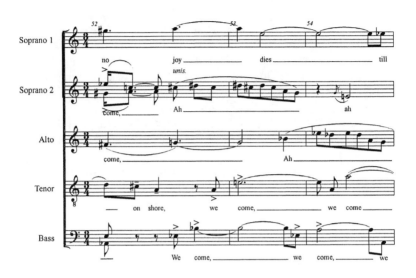

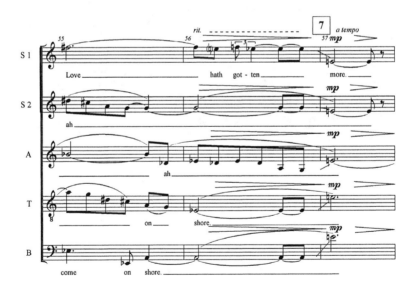

Creatures

In her two sets of miniatures, written in the late 1970s, Maconchy chose poems by British authors especially well-known for writing children's verse. Eleanor Farjeon (1881-1965) is the sole poet for the set *Four Miniatures*, a work for SATB choir, commissioned by the Broadland Singers. Farjeon also contributed one poem to the set of seven in *Creatures*. Other poets, all but one contemporary, are William Blake (1757-1827), E. V. Rieu (1887-1972), Ian Serraillier (1912-1994) and James Reeves (1909-1978). *Creatures* was commissioned by Stephen Wilkinson and the BBC Northern Singers. Though composed as sets, pieces from either cycle may be performed individually.

 Creatures consists of seven short, lighthearted pieces, ingeniously affectionate animal portraits from Blake's noble tiger to the humble snail, rounded off by a whirlwind chase of a dog in pursuit of a cat that ends as suddenly as it began. The text for "The Snail," second in the set, is by James Reeves, who writes short poems with dancing rhythms and nonsense syllables. He captures quickly the picture of the snail's journey in search of food. In forty measures Maconchy too captures the scene of the snail at sunset, as she silently "clambers down carrying her house of brown." The music expands and contracts to reflect the movements of this little creature as it searches for the freshest leaf.

 The altos enter alone, humming an ostinato that recurs every measure in alto, tenor, or bass voices. The ostinato centers around A, with new pitches added every several beats. The tenors enter in m. 2, also humming, but their notes are sustained, and they are encouraged to slide from pitch to pitch, *portamento sempre* (Example 3.11). This motive, centered on F, appears in tenor or bass throughout most of the piece. The opening measures sound polymodal: each line avoids pitches that are being used in the other voices.

Example 3.11. *Creatures*, "The Snail," mm. 1-4.

For the first ten measures the sopranos alone carry the text; the snail's story unfolds in their lyrical line. In m. 13 the altos join the sopranos and together they deliver the rest of the tale. Individual lines represent characterizations of the snail as part of the text-painting. The independent lines become complex when combined, and Maconchy's use of chromaticism within individual lines creates a polymodal flavor. A moment of delightful text-painting occurs in mm. 33-35, when descending sevenths, one after another, depict the snail's movements: "She travels on as best she can, Like a toppling caravan" (Example 3.12).

Example 3.12. *Creatures*, "The Snail," mm. 33-36.

"Cat!" by Eleanor Farjeon is the text for the final piece in *Creatures*. It comes from one of her many books for children, *Sing for Your Supper*. As colibrettist of an opera produced by the Royal Academy of Music and publisher of several dozen books for children, Farjeon is as familiar to English youngsters as A. A. Milne is to American. Her themes are traditional, but her treatment of them is original and imaginative. "Cat!" is about an active alley cat, sleek, scratching and scritching the bark of a tree, as she is pursued by a dog in a mad chase.

All voices begin together on a unison D[4], "Cat!" The half-note is accented and marked *fp* with a crescendo that moves to a *forte*, accented trichord on "Scat!" With great economy Maconchy introduces the compositional material she will use for this fifty-four measure portrait. The trichord in m. 2 consists of a fifth, a half-step, and a tritone and punctuates the texture throughout. A three-note descending melodic pattern that appears in m. 3 is the main material to be repeated and developed throughout the piece (Example 3.13). Another recurring pattern that peppers the score is the two-note descending interval in m. 4, in the soprano voice.

Example 3.13. *Creatures*, "Cat!" mm. 1-5.

The secondal relationships that can be detected in the squirrelly, descending motives are a device reminiscent of Bartók. Contrapuntal texture pervades the score, with two-part imitation and frequent voice pairing. The three-note figure is presented in a variety of ways: transposed up a step, fragmented, extended, and augmented. The measures of augmentation illustrate "slithery," notated in an effective hemiola, sung *legato*, just before a tetrachord, one of the few in the piece (Example 3.14). Maconchy matches every word with an appropriate sound picture.

Example 3.14. *Creatures*, "Cat!" mm. 17-22.

Maconchy uses a new sort of notation for descriptive animal sounds. In "Cat!" the words "Wuff!" and "Pfitts!" are written under vertical lines that indicate duration but not pitch. Two of these occur just before the final measures of the piece, which ends on the unison D^4 (Example 3.15).

Example 3.15. *Creatures*, "Cat!" mm. 47-54.

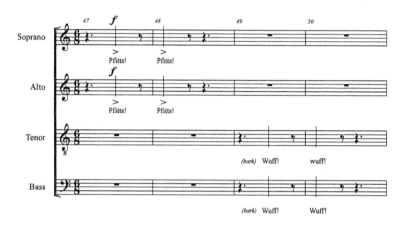

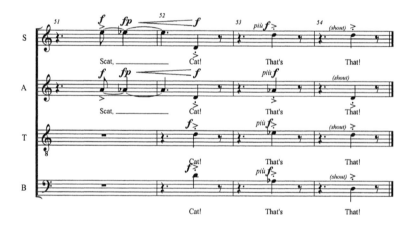

Lesser Works

The majority of Maconchy's accompanied choral works are for choir and small instrumental ensemble; the exception is *Heloise and Abelard* (1977), a cantata for STB soloists, chorus, and full orchestra. The twelfth-century story of Abelard and Heloise has inspired a vast body of fictional and historical literature. However, Maconchy chose to write her own libretto, patterning it on primary sources. In her version the action revolves around Heloise and her relationship with Abelard, and thus much of the libretto is taken from Heloise's letters. There is ample writing for chorus, and between the hymns, plainchants, and laments, the love story unfolds in quasi-operatic style.

> The work opens most impressively with a sonorously jubilant setting of Abelard's Easter hymn "Veris grato tempore" and every subsequent appearance of the chorus immediately evokes an appropriate emotional response. The seductive lilt of the students' love song "admirabile Veneris idolum" for example, or the gently lulling rhythms of women's "Sleep sound, little one," which forms a magical background for Heloise's lullaby. . . . But what gives the work its most intense and lasting aural enchantment is beautiful and endlessly imaginative treatment of the orchestra, which creates a constantly changing kaleidoscope of richly colourful and appealing sound patterns.[29]

The earliest accompanied pieces in Maconchy's choral renaissance are *Christmas Morning* (1962) and "The Armado" (1962). The first is a carol cantata intended for girls', boys', or women's chorus, with soprano soloist and piano or organ accompaniment. It has also been scored for recorders or other woodwinds, bells, cymbal, two timpani, and piano. It consists of original settings of six carols linked by a brief narration of the Christmas story, given to the solo voice.

"The Armado" is a light, humorous ballad: a story to be sung, for mixed chorus and piano. The verses were written by an anonymous author about the fight and defeat of the Spanish Armada by Sir Francis Drake and the English. A charming rhyme is used when the final "a" in Armada is changed in order to rhyme "Armado" with "Bravado." Folk songs, usually written in strophic form, are often set with the same music accompanying all verses. Maconchy creates real interest in the vocal lines by adding variety to each verse. All eight verses are quite different. There are other humorous word changes that contribute to the light and conversational tone of this work.

Maconchy set Dylan Thomas' *And Death Shall Have No Dominion* (1969) for choir, treble solo, and brass consort of two horns, three trumpets, and three trombones. Written for the Three Choirs Festival at Worchester Cathedral, Maconchy showed a keen awareness for cathedral acoustics. Again, her compositional traits of economy and tautly fashioned writing from materials introduced in the opening measures is evident here.

Some of Maconchy's finest settings have been those to words by Gerard Manley Hopkins (1844-1889). During the late 1970s she set three of Hopkins' most lyrical poems for soprano and chamber orchestra: "A Starlight Night," "Peace," and "The May Magnificat." In her *Two Settings* of poems by Gerard Manley Hopkins for choir and brass (two horns, two trumpets, and three trombones), she set "Pied Beauty" and "Heaven-Haven." The pieces were written for Richard Seal and the Choir of Salisbury Cathedral and are beautifully contrasted, sensitive, lyrical settings of Hopkins' jewel-like poems. Her finest and most frequently performed choral work is *The Leaden Echo and the Golden Echo* (1978) for chorus, alto flute, viola, and harp.

The Leaden Echo and the Golden Echo

Gerard Manley Hopkins was an English Jesuit priest and poet whose most important poetry is religious. He is known for using "sprung rhythm," which he described as the rhythm of common speech and written prose, and "the rhythm of all but the most monotonously regular music."[30] It is unlike traditional poetry, which has a number of regular feet per line and where the reader supplies the underlying pattern and then notes the variations from its standard. Hopkins uses no fixed stress pattern. There can be any number of syllables per line, with unstressed syllables usually clustering around stressed syllables. Sprung rhythm has order: the scansion is by the fixed number of stresses per line. Since Hopkins intended his poems to be heard, not read, alliteration, internal and end-rhyme, assonance, and similar devices are important. Though sometimes used ornamentally, they always carry meaning.

Completed in 1882, *The Leaden Echo and the Golden Echo* was intended as part of a play called *St. Winefred's Well*, a work that was never finished. The poem was to have been a chorus of St. Winefred's Maidens, possibly a finale to the drama.[31] Hopkins meant the poem to be sung, and said he had never written anything more musical.[32]

"The Leaden Echo" consists of sixteen lines, followed by the reply of "The Golden Echo" in thirty-two lines. The poems are examples of Greek drama's strophe and antistrophe—one echo talks, another replies. The first echo asks the question, whereas the second reverses it and answers it. The poem uses pure sprung rhythm in varying line lengths, of from two to twelve stresses per line.

Two attitudes are posed by the echoes in the paired poems. "The Leaden Echo" is heavy; it mourns and laments the fleeting nature of physical beauty. It is reversed by "The Golden Echo," which states that becoming unduly attached to beauty leads to despair. "The Golden Echo" advises giving beauty back to God, who gave it originally, because nothing is lost to God: "Give beauty back, beauty, beauty, beauty, back to God, beauty's self and beauty's giver." Thus beauty can be saved, and man with it.

Hopkins enjoys the sheer pleasure of words tumbling vibrantly over one another. A type of alliterative displacement occurs frequently: for example, in the second line of text: "*bow* or *br*ooch or *bra*id or *bra*ce, *lace*, *latch* or *catch* or *key* to *keep*." Alliterative patterns are established, which are followed by sequential displacements. Notice how the phoneme "b" is common in the beginning. It expands to "br" and then "bra," which is followed by a rhyme, "brace, lace." Finally the alliteration moves to the last part of the word. Displacement of the alliteration itself creates a chain of melodious sounds. Another example of sequential displacement from "The Golden Echo" is "sweet looks, loose locks, long locks, lovelocks," then "gaygear, going gallant, girlgrace."

Another kind of displacement Hopkins uses in *The Leaden Echo and the Golden Echo* is a grammatic one, where extra material, either adjectives or alliterative units, is added in the middle of a sentence. The following lines open "The Leaden Echo":

How to keep—is there any any, is there none such, nowhere known some, bow or
brooch or braid or brace, lace, latch or catch or key to keep
Back beauty, keep is, beauty, beauty, beauty . . . from vanishing away?

The idea posed in this opening passage is "how to keep beauty from vanishing away?" The immediate text expands on the basic idea in a way that is not unlike the development of a motive in music. This is an example of Hopkins' musical approach to his text. When read aloud, the meaning can be grasped, even though the sentence has been interrupted.

Hopkins ends "The Leaden Echo" with a series of echoes on the word "despair." The overall effect is one of heaviness, darkness, and depression. "The Golden Echo" opens with the word "Spare!" (meaning listen), a telling rhyme that functions as a contrast and remedy to the leaden despair of the first poem.

When the thing we freely forfeit is kept with fonder a care,
Fonder a care kept than we could keep it, kept
Far with fonder a care (and we, we should have lost it) finer, fonder,
A care kept.—Where kept? Do but tell us where kept, where.-
Yonder.—What high as that! We follow, now we follow.—
Yonder, yes yonder, yonder,
Yonder.

Maconchy's evocative and sensitive setting of Hopkins' *The Leaden Echo and the Golden Echo* was premiered by the William Byrd Singers of Manchester, Stephen Wilkinson conducting, on November 25, 1978. It is scored for mixed chorus, which must be large enough to accommodate frequent divisi in all parts. There are several short phrases written for SSAT soloists, most of which appear in the second poem. There is also a substantial solo for first soprano. Instrumental accompaniment is assigned to the sensuous combination of alto flute, viola, and harp.

Maconchy uses a slow harmonic rhythm. This enables her to draw attention to the alliteration in the text. The repetitions and sequential word patterns create long sentences. Hopkins achieves a sense of timelessness in his text, and Maconchy's choice of harmonic language reinforces it, another example of her sensitivity in text-setting. There is no stable tonal center: tonal ambiguity and free chromaticism dominate the harmonic language more than is the case in *Nocturnal* or "Siren's Song." Maconchy uses a modified octatonic scale in which leading tones and dominants are consciously avoided and tritones permeate the texture. There are occasional transpositions to provide some sense of tonal motion, but the pitch collection is basically the same.

Throughout Maconchy's choral works, the rhythm serves the text. The natural accentuation of the text is followed closely, and text declamation is clear: the rhythmic treatment is straightforward. Maconchy avoids frequent meter changes to accommodate the stresses and accents of the text, relying instead on rhythmic divisions within the measure. Occasionally, a measure in 3/4 or 5/4 appears, but the piece is primarily in common time. Maconchy understands the demands of setting sprung rhythms, with their irregular stress patterns and abundant repetitions.

Maconchy's sensitivity to text-setting is apparent in her clarity and expressivity and complete understanding of Hopkins' already musical setting. The challenge of setting the grammatic displacement, for example, might present a difficult problem owing to the amount of musical time that might elapse before the complete phrase has been presented. Maconchy has been able to summarize, then foreshadow the essence of the phrase, while honoring the repetition and sequential word patterns of the text. Example 3.16 illustrates how the words and music work together, and how Maconchy sensitively reacts to the sounds of the text while also conveying meaning.

Example 3.16. *The Leaden Echo and the Golden Echo*, mm 9-18.

The next challenge in setting text is confronting the changes in pace or tempo within the text itself. On her approach to matching the variety of pace within the poem, Machonchy comments: "There are lines that hurry forward propelled by an almost aggressive alliteration followed by lines of slowly drawn out syllables. In music the two can happen at the same time, something which music can do, which words alone cannot."[33]

A vivid example of her solution and musical reworking is found in mm. 202-210, where the upper voices move in slow chords, while the lower voices move at a faster pace (Example 3.17). The text in the upper voices, "what while we slept," is sung *piano* and marked *tranquillo sempre*, while the lower parts sing "this side, that side, hurling a heavyheaded hundredfold," marked *poco forte, vigoroso*. Two different tempos appear to occur and two different lines are presented simultaneously.

Example 3.17. *The Leaden Echo and the Golden Echo*, mm. 202-208.

The dialogue between the echoes is reflected in Maconchy's musical setting. In mm. 236-239, for example, "The Leaden Echo" asks where God keeps beauty, "where kept?" The sopranos, in three-part divisi, sing "where kept? Do but tell us where kept?" *pianissimo*, "echo tone" (Example 3.18).

Example 3.18. *The Leaden Echo and the Golden Echo*, mm. 235-238.

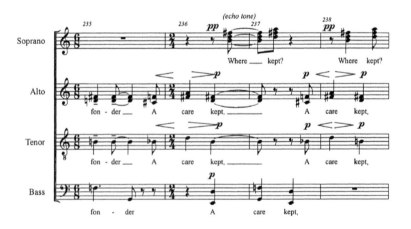

While generally considered a conservative composer, Maconchy is not opposed to new techniques. Between rehearsal numbers 17 and 18 there is only one long measure that is asynchronous (Example 3.19). The women are instructed: "all sing, choosing from the phrases at will, and unsynchronized." This is yet another example of Maconchy's musical setting serving the text. The text is saying youth is its own best beauty, its own essence. Hopkins uses another series of sensuous sounds—"Winning ways, airs innocent, maiden manners, sweet looks, loose locks, long locks, lovelocks, gaygear, going gallant, girlgrace"—which fall over one another like the voices in Maconchy's setting.

Example 3.19. *The Leaden Echo and the Golden Echo*, rehearsal 17.

In 1987, Maconchy's eightieth year, she became the second woman to receive the honor of Dame of the British Empire:[34]

> In this year of her eightieth birthday hundreds of musicians have written to her paying tribute to her integrity, courage, dedication, vitality, and enthusiasm. The best tribute comes in the many performances of her music, both from players who have always championed her and in particular from the new generation of young instrumentalists who are now discovering how rewarding her music is. Elizabeth Maconchy has always kept abreast of contemporary thought, while pursuing her own path, never swayed by modish conventions.[35]

While chiefly known for her thirteen string quartets and other chamber music, Maconchy wrote many choral works in her last years that deserve attention. She wrote music practical for children's voices and music for high school, college, and professional groups. Each concert in a recent series of contemporary music programs by the BBC Singers contained a substantial choral work by Maconchy. Her choral works receive frequent performances, and her music is very popular with singers.

> It doesn't get any easier with the years. But I compose because I have to. . . . After a blank patch now and then the urge to write has up till now returned again with its old compulsion—ideas begin to come, and one is off again, planning, writing, scrapping—with a mounting pile of manuscript on the floor. Being a composer is a life-sentence from which there is no escape.[36]

Notes

1. John Skiba, "In Conversation with Elizabeth Maconchy," *Composer* 63 (Spring 1978): 7.

2. Anne Macnaghten, "Elizabeth Maconchy," *Musical Times* 96 (June 1955): 298.

3. Elizabeth Maconchy, "A Composer Speaks," *Composer* 42 (Winter 1971-1972): 25.

4. Skiba, "In Conversation," 7.

5. Skiba, "In Conversation," 9.

6. Karel Boleslav Jirák (1891-1972) was a Czech composer and conductor who toured extensively throughout Europe, performing and promoting Czech music. He was a prominent administrator in the ISCM. In 1947 he moved to the United States.

7. Maconchy, "A Composer Speaks," 25.

8. Brochure from J & W Chester Music, 1978.

9. In a short article published in the *RCM Magazine* (Autumn 1987) celebrating her mother's Dame of the British Empire honor, Nicola LeFanu wrote, "When it [*The Land*] was performed in 1987 at one of the concerts in honour of her eightieth birthday, the audience rose at the end in a standing ovation—a rare accolade in this country. It is a sad comment on the conformity of our musical establishment that it has not become a part of the standard repertory."

10. Constant Lambert, quoted by Roger Wright, in "A Talk with Elizabeth Maconchy," BBC Radio Broadcast, n.d.

11. The other women involved in the founding of the Macnaghten-Lemare Concert Series were Iris Lemare and Anne Macnaghten. (See chapter 2 for more information.)

12. Anne Macnaghten, "Composer's Portrait," Interview with Elisabeth Maconchy for BBC Radio, n.d; John Skiba, "In Conversation," 7.

13. The Composer's Guild of Great Britain began in London in the late 1940s. The group founded the British Music Information Centre (BMIC), the Guild's Reference Library of contemporary British scores, tapes, and recordings at 10 Stratford Place, London W1. *Composer* is published quarterly by the Guild through the BMIC.

14. Benjamin Britten wrote three string quartets, Michael Tippett wrote four, and Elisabeth Lutyens wrote six.

15. Maconchy, "A Composer Speaks," 28.

16. Maconchy, "A Composer Speaks," 28.

17. Elizabeth Maconchy, "Composer's Portrait," BBC Radio Interview, n.d.

18. *The New Grove Dictionary of Music and Musicians*, s.v. "Elizabeth Maconchy," by Hugo Cole.

19. Elizabeth Maconchy, "A Composer Speaks," 28.

20. Elizabeth Maconchy, paraphrased from the film *Elizabeth Maconchy*, directed by Margaret Williams, 1985. Produced by the Arts Council of Great Britain.

21. Elizabeth Maconchy, paraphrased from the film *Elizabeth Maconchy*, directed by Margaret Williams, 1985. Produced by the Arts Council of Great Britain.

22. See Appendix F for a complete, chronological listing of Maconchy's choral works.

23. *Two Motets* and *Six Yeats Settings* remain in manuscript. Both, however, are available from St. Hilda's College, Oxford, and may be performed.

24. Elizabeth Maconchy, program note for the "BBC Singers in Twentieth-Century Music," a concert series from April to June 1987, held at St. John's Smith Square.

25. See Appendix G for the text of *Nocturnal*.

26. Also called the Bartók Scale, the gapped scale consists of alternating minor thirds and minor seconds.

27. A masque is a form of dramatic entertainment with music, popular among the aristocracy in England during the sixteenth and seventeenth centuries. Usually, it was based on a mythical or allegorical theme and was written in verse.

28. See Appendix H for the text of "Siren's Song."

29. Roger Harris, "Heloise and Abelard," *Music and Musicians* 27 (1979): 58-59.

30. Gerard Manley Hopkins quoted in Roger Wright, "Maconchy," a talk by Roger Wright for the BBC, n.d.

31. According to the later medieval legend, St. Winefred (a Welsh virgin martyr) was a niece of St. Beuno. Her head was cut off by Cardoc, the chieftain's son, whose sexual advances she had resisted. Beuno restored the head to her body, and where the head had fallen (at Holywell, near St. Beuno's), a spring of healing water appeared. King Henry VII's mother, Lady Margaret Beaufort, had the well enclosed by a stone building, and it remains a place of pilgrimage.

32. See Appendix I for the complete text of *The Leaden Echo and the Golden Echo*.

33. See Appendix I.

34. The first was Dame Ethel Smyth.

35. Nicola LeFanu, "Elizabeth Maconchy," *RCM Magazine* (Autumn 1987): 114.

36. Maconchy, "A Composer Speaks," 29.

Thea Musgrave (1928-)

Thea Musgrave was born in Barnton, Midlothian, near Edinburgh, Scotland, on May 27, 1928. Music was an essential part of her childhood. She recalls, "I was always composing little snatches of this and that."[1] Yet it was not until she had begun a premedical course at Edinburgh University in 1947 that she irrevocably chose a life in music. During her undergraduate years she studied piano, harmony, and analysis under Mary Gardner Grierson, and counterpoint, music history, and composition with Austrian composer Hans Gál. In 1950 she received her Bachelor of Music degree and was awarded the Donald Francis Tovey Prize. Encouraged by pianist Lucille Wallace and enabled by a postgraduate scholarship, she studied in France from 1950 to 1954 with Nadia Boulanger, both at the Paris Conservatoire and as a private pupil. From Boulanger, Musgrave learned the fundamental principles of discipline and economy and "the importance of every bar,"[2] as Musgrave acknowledged. Of her work with Boulanger, Musgrave continues:

> It wasn't the piano accompaniment class; we never did any accompanying on the piano, but it was much more. We did score reading, figured bass, transposition, and of course, studied Stravinsky. It was a wonderful general music education.[3]

Allen Sapp's observation of Musgrave's formative years and her surrounding, nurturing environment is enlightening:

> These were the molding years—in many ways known best only to her, the formative twenty years along the strip adjacent to the Firth of Forth, the incubation in a very conservative town such as Edinburgh; the cosmopolitanizing encounter of Paris, which in the early 1950s was assessing the impact of the Second Viennese School, the place of pioneering experiments in *musique concréte*, the return from imprisonment of Olivier Messiaen and his potent role as a teacher and composer

(*Turangalîla* for example) against the whole backdrop of a France losing its empire; savagely engaged in a desperate moral, political, and military struggle; and the startup of a flow of composing opportunities, commissions, festivals, fellowships and the like. All these times and places helped to catalyze a steady flow of musical compositions beginning in 1952 and continuing on to the present with a latent but discernible force. For in the music of the first decade, there is much of the essential composer.[4]

In 1952 Musgrave received the coveted Lili Boulanger Memorial Prize in composition, the first Scottish composer to be so honored. In 1953 she fulfilled her first commission—from the Scottish Festival at Braemar—with *A Suite O'Bairnsangs* for voice and piano. Other early works in a predominately tonal and lyrical style were *Four Madrigals* for unaccompanied chorus and a ballet, *A Tale of Three Thieves*. The following year, 1954, BBC Scotland commissioned *Cantata for a Summer's Day*, scored for chamber ensemble, narrator, and small chorus, a work often referred to as her first major success. In 1955 Musgrave returned to live in London, where her music had already aroused interest, and she began to receive a number of commissions. She also became coach-accompanist for the London-based Saltire Singers, with whom she concertized and toured, mainly in Scotland but also England and Europe. This group was to commission and perform several works by her.

Beginning in 1955, her works show a gradual movement toward serial technique. Her chromaticism was still anchored by tonal centers, but her melodic lines became angular and less easily singable. Musgrave's first fully serial piece was a setting for high voice and piano of "A Song of Christmas," a declamatory dramatic scena written in 1958. This was followed by the colorful "Triptych" for tenor and orchestra, commissioned by the Saltire Society in 1959. Other instrumental works using serial techniques show her personal adaptation of the twelve-tone system; however, she wrote no choral works using this technique. Musgrave's strict serial phase lasted no more than two years. Andrew Porter commented at the time:

> Although she thinks it is irrelevant in the first instance, to ask if a composer belongs to the 12-tone school or not, since that is purely a technical matter, she however has found that the 12-tone technique, far from being restrictive, has led to new thematic and structural possibilities, new harmonies, new instrumental colors, and a far wider range of expression than she would have believed possible.[5]

Although Musgrave was living in London, commissions continued to come to her from Scottish patrons, including the BBC, the Scottish Opera, the Saltire Society, and others, and Musgrave has regularly turned to Scottish poets and subjects in her choral and operatic works.

While three well-written, substantial choral works—*The Phoenix and the Turtle*, *The Five Ages of Man*, and *Marko the Miser*—were completed between 1961 and 1965, this period marks a break in Musgrave's development. Without commission or prospect of performance, she embarked on her first full-length opera, *The Decision*, and worked on it for two years, to the virtual exclusion of everything else. The libretto, by Maurice Lindsay, was based on a true incident that occurred in Scotland in 1835, involving a trapped Scots miner and the attempts made to rescue him. The ensuing tragedy prompted labor laws for new safety conditions in Scottish mines. The world premiere of *The Decision* in 1967 at Sadler's Wells in London was a success. As Stephen Walsh wrote:

> This was her biggest undertaking to date and for all the prevailing somberness appropriate to the subject of a mining accident and the conflicting moral dilemmas in which it places those involved, its magic shows a marked enrichment of both expressive and technical means. *The Decision* forced an extroversion which earlier works had generally lacked, and the benefit is apparent in most of Musgrave's subsequent work.[6]

The Decision led Musgrave in a new direction as a composer. She became preoccupied with an instrumental style she describes as dramatic-abstract: dramatic in the sense that certain instruments take on the character of dramatic personages, and abstract because there is no program. Of the approximately twenty-seven instrumental compositions written between 1964 and 1972, many are concerti based on the working out of a dramatic confrontation. While each part is fully notated, it need not be exactly coordinated with others or with the conductor; such a technique is described as asynchronous music. Musgrave explains:

> It seemed to me that, to realize the full potential of the soloists, they would at times have to be independent of the bar-line, and also at times, independent of the conductor. I wanted to have moments of freedom of expression without the texture of the whole lapsing into anarchy. I therefore evolved a system of intercueing the parts where the players play in relation to one another, occasionally giving each other leads. At certain dramatic moments, I asked the soloists to stand, as I am convinced this encourages them to play with greater virtuosity and furthermore heightens the tension, as the standing implies a certain defiance of the conductor. The confrontation became part of the dramatic form.[7]

The system of intercueing the parts and Musgrave's solutions in new instrumental dramatic forms can be seen in the Concerto for Orchestra and the Clarinet Concerto. Freedom and excitement emerge in performance when various instruments play cadenzas at the same time, where some instrumentalists play in strict tempo while others play freely, and where at least two different, nonrelated tempos occur simultaneously but with no loss of harmonic control. Musgrave relates:

> In some of my early lyrical works such as *A Suite O'Bairnsangs* and *A Cantata for a Summer's Day*, melodic ideas had an important role, indeed they seemed to me vital. But in most of my recent works, though they are not void of melodic content, the starting point has been a dramatic formal shape, which has often come to in a vivid flash, though not quite in the way described by Hindemith—

that is, complete in every detail. On the contrary, these ideas have usually been of a general nature with at the same time, a concept of total form. The act of composing was therefore an exploration and not just a working-out: the form was flexible enough, while retaining its dramatic structure, to allow room for unexpected developments.[8]

During this period Musgrave did not write a single song or opera. However, she did write one choral work, "Memento Creatoris." Scored for SAT soloists, mixed chorus, and organ ad lib., the piece displays a dramatic, virtuosic style with contrapuntal and rhythmic demands on individual sections in the chorus.

Acoustics and spatial separation of ensembles for quasi-theatrical reasons are of interest to Musgrave. Several of her compositions, such as *Space Play* and portions of the Concerto for Horn, make imaginative use of spatial relationships. Performers stand at some distance from each other, or move about the stage, and when performing with the orchestra, are to join in different orchestral sections from time to time.

A natural outgrowth of Musgrave's interest in the dramatic aspects of instrumental music was her return, in 1973, to operatic composition. In *The Voice of Ariadne*, a three-act chamber opera, the asynchronous techniques of the concerti are carried over into the vocal ensembles. Thus reinvigorating opera by giving new roles to the operatic ensemble, she relies on tradition and infuses it with contemporary techniques and her own ideas. Musgrave's views are amplified by her librettist, Amalia Elguera, who adds:

> Ensemble, far from being old fashioned, strikes me as a modern, perspectivist form: the lightening up of a dramatic object or objective from different subjective angles. In the time arts, ensemble alone fully achieves the simultaneity which otherwise belongs to the arts of space.[9]

In addition, Musgrave gives an important role to electronic sounds. *The Voice of Ariadne*, based on a short story by Henry James and dedicated to Benjamin Britten, is essentially a romantic ghost story. It portrays a husband who is temporarily seduced by a voice from a statue of Ariadne, which only he can hear. Although he becomes enamored of the voice, he finally realizes that his wife is his only true love. The voice of Ariadne, along with sounds suggesting the sea and other effects, are supplied on prerecorded tape. Musgrave explains:

> I found it very interesting that use of tape can lift you to another level, that it has real dramatic force. . . . What attracted me was the character who wasn't there— a statue. I think subconsciously I have been looking for something in which tape could be used, and when I found the statue, I thought, my God, this is it. . . . I recorded the voice so that the words can always be clearly understood and what I've done at certain moments is to superimpose several voices with an echo effect, and add electronic sounds suggesting the sea and distance.[10]

Musgrave, though aware of tradition, is innovative in a contemporary context while maintaining sensitivity to vocal requirements. Her writing is demanding, but technical challenges always are within natural limits and not just doing something for its own sake, and she always produces an idiomatic result.

> Her score is a natural flowering from the new freedoms, the adventurousness, and the lyrical delight in sound and gesture which she showed in previous orchestral pieces. It is very well written for singers: the rightness in matching emotional pitch to actual tessitura, the sense of where in the voice to find a particular shade of feeling, the naturalness of the declamation, and the unstrained transition from conversation to formal set pieces all tell of a born opera composer.[11]

Although Musgrave has as yet written no choral piece using electronic media, one of her most descriptive, colorful, and dramatic choral works, *Rorate Coeli*, dates from the same year as *Ariade*. The same asynchronous techniques are employed in this extended unaccompanied work for five soloists and mixed choir. While *The Last Twilight*, an accompanied choral piece with brass and percussion written several years after *Rorate Coeli*, makes no use of asynchronous techniques, this theater piece involves a number of dramatic techniques, including scenery and staging for the chorus. Like *Rorate Coeli*, *The Last Twilight* makes use of rich, sonorous effects within the textures, yet permits the all-important text to be understood.

In the early 1970s, Musgrave came to the United States as a visiting professor of music at the University of California at Santa Barbara. While teaching composition there she met another faculty member, New York-born violist Peter Mark, and they were married in London in 1971. They now divide their time between Santa Barbara and Norfolk, Virginia, where Mark is general director and conductor of the Virginia Opera Association.

During the late 1970s Musgrave wrote two operas, *Mary Queen of Scots* (1977), one of her most significant works to date, and *A Christmas Carol* (1979), probably her most frequently performed work. When commissioned to write *Mary*, Musgrave confessed: "Really I'm the right person; because I'm Scots, I'm a woman, I was educated in France, I'm tall . . . but I haven't got red hair."[12]

Mary is a straightforward treatment of a historical subject. Musgrave's own libretto is based on a historical play by Amalia Elguera, in which Mary, eighteen years old and already the widow of the king of France, returns to Scotland in 1561 to assume the throne. She is sent away seven years later to England by her half-brother, the earl of Moray. The opera's musical idiom is accessible and often tonal and incorporates dances of the period. The orchestral textures are always inventive, and the chorus is used very resourcefully, on and off stage. After the American premiere in 1978, Andrew Porter wrote:

> It is an interesting, affecting and important work, successful on many counts: as a poetic drama, as representation of characters and conflicts, as a study of history, as a long stretch of imagination and excellently written music, and as a music

drama in which words, sounds, spectacle and action conspire to stir a listener's mind and emotion. In short, it succeeds as a show, as a score, and as that fusion of both which creates good opera.[13]

A Christmas Carol, Musgrave's first opera written and premiered in the United States, is based on Charles Dickens' classic. Again, Musgrave wrote her own libretto, and her score calls for twelve soloists, an orchestra of fifteen, and an optional children's chorus at the end. Annalyn Swan, reviewing *Carol*, observed:

> The opera sparkles with Dickensian humor and good cheer. . . . Musgrave's characteristic dissonance with its echoes here and there of Benjamin Britten, undermines Scrooge's misanthropy. But, as befits the sentimental theme, Musgrave has created the most melodic of her five operas. She even decorates some passages with intervals of thirds and fifths, the harmonies so beloved by the nineteenth century and eschewed by the twentieth.[14]

Her opera *Harriet, the Woman Called Moses* (1985) is based on the life of Harriet Tubman, whose exploits as a conductor on the Underground Railroad that smuggled slaves to freedom in Canada before the Civil War made her a major heroine in American history. Musgrave's score for *Harriet* makes use of authentic tunes, folk songs, and spirituals, as she tells of Harriet's escape from slavery and the many people who helped her. The work opens and closes with a thundering chorus built around two chords that carry the "freedom" leitmotiv of the opera. The chorus is almost always on stage to observe, comment on, or participate in the action. Patrick Smith remarked:

> Each of Musgrave's operas has shown an increasingly sure grasp of musical drama, and a paring of her music to essentials. She knows how to set a scene and build to a climax, and she uses the many folk tunes—here, Negro spirituals, especially "Go Down Moses" and its final line "let my people go"—with subtlety and expertise, weaving them into counterpoint to the rest of the music. This use of folk material has always been a Musgrave trademark: in *Harriet* it is its best.[15]

In addition to Musgrave's accomplishments as a pianist, composer, and lecturer, she has become a respected conductor of her own works. The third woman to conduct the Philadelphia Orchestra since its inception in 1900,[16] she was also the first to conduct her own composition, the Concerto for Orchestra. She has directed the New York City Opera, the Los Angeles Chamber Orchestra, the San Diego and San Francisco Symphony Orchestras, the St. Paul Chamber Orchestra, the BBC Symphony Orchestra, and the Royal Philharmonic.

Musgrave is fortunate in having had almost all her works performed soon after they were written. She recognizes what a valuable lesson this is for any composer, for only then can she gain confidence and begin to explore new and individual paths:

I was very fortunate. Coming from Scotland, many of my early works were premiered by the BBC Scotland, conducted by Colin Davis. Then, when I moved to London, my music was performed by the BBC in London. To be able to start a career under these conditions is absolutely fabulous.[17]

Musgrave's early style period spans the years 1953 to 1957. Her studies with Boulanger, which proved to be an artistic awakening for Musgrave, reinforced the concern for detail and economy that is apparent in the works of these years. The harmonic language is clearly tonal; the melodic lines move principally in conjunct motion in a lyric, singable style. Musgrave uses a great deal of flexibility in her choice of rhythmic and metrical structures. Her music of this period also displays her concern for clarity in setting text. In addition, these early works indicate a total familiarity with compositional styles from the past. As Musgrave has observed:

Everything's been done before. The thing about tradition is to use it. Naturally, as a composer you don't want to copy something because it's been done successfully, but you can take what you need from the past and rethink it in an entirely fresh way.[18]

Musgrave's choral music may be divided into four categories: works for unaccompanied chorus, works for chorus with organ, works for chorus with chamber-sized ensemble, and works for chorus with orchestra.[19]

Four Madrigals

Four Madrigals, Musgrave's earliest choral composition, belongs in the first category and shows her sensitivity to text-setting and her interest in the late Renaissance madrigal. Like many of her sixteenth-century models, the subject matter of these madrigals is love—suitors speaking of the loves, posturing, teasing, all tongue-in-cheek and not to be taken too seriously. Musgrave chose four poems by Sir Thomas Wyatt (1503-1542), an English poet who was fascinated with Italy and Italian Renaissance writers. The lover in the Italian sonnets chosen to be set as madrigals was usually in a mood of doleful despair; the typical poem is essentially a complaint. Wyatt reflects this in his text "At Most Mischief," Musgrave's third madrigal. The injured suitor, having no relief, plays his lute and suffers.

At most mischief
I suffer grief
For of relief
Since I have none
My lute and I
Continually
Shall us apply

To sigh and moan
. . . .
Naught do ye care
How I smart.

Musically, the sixteenth-century madrigal, while undergoing a number of stylistic developments, was essentially a multisectional work employing contrasting textures without relying on strict formal structures. Its primary aim was to present its text in the clearest, most appropriate, and most expressive manner. Musgrave reflects these characteristics in her own set of four-part madrigals. In the first madrigal, "With serving still," there are frequent meter changes in order to create a natural delineation of the text. Voices are often used in combinations of two and three, so that for at least half the piece, only three voices sound at one time. Short, descending motives reflect the pathos of such phrases of the text as "to be undone," "of all my pain," "of all my smart," and "as I am thrall" (Example 4.1).

Example 4.1. *Four Madrigals*, "With serving still," mm. 1-10.

The writing is succinct, and repetition of the text appears only in the seven-measure coda. Although the scansion of each stanza is identical, the five short strophes are through-composed. In the last three measures of the final stanza, Musgrave quotes her opening three measures exactly and uses this motivic material to construct the seven-measure extension (Example 4.2).

Example 4.2. *Four Madrigals*, "With serving still," mm. 30-41.

Musgrave uses only two of the six stanzas of "tanglid I was in loves' snare," and they are set strophically. Texturally imitating the style of a chanson, alto, tenor, and bass voices are subordinate to the main melodic line. The ornamented soprano part, with text-painting on descriptive words—"tanglid," "pain," and "grief"—delivers the expressive content of the text (Example 4.3).

Example 4.3. *Four Madrigals*, "Tanglid I was in love's snare," mm. 1-4.

This madrigal differs from others in the set. The contrasting sections marked *andante* and *vivo* underscore the lover's obsession. Languid, *legato* lines are used to create a doleful, despairing mood at the beginning of each stanza, while the *vivo* section, marked *leggiero*, is light and sprightly, using a recurrent, homophonic "ha-ha" refrain to demonstrate the suitor's newfound freedom, "for now I am at libertye." Polymodality is consistently used in the opening section, as each individual vocal line is oriented to a different mode and pitch. E phrygian, in particular, plays an important role in the *vivo* section. As in the other madrigals in the set, Musgrave does not stay with any one tonality or mode. There is a certain variety of pitch centers throughout the madrigal in both the tonality as a whole and within individual vocal lines. In the more contrapuntal sections, the chords are a by-product of the short melodic lines, reflecting Renaissance practice.

At the beginning of "At most mischief," the third madrigal, Musgrave achieves a sense of intimacy by using imitation in the soprano and alto voices. The languid melodic lines are typical of her lyric style during this period and contain many modal inflections. In the opening bars, the sopranos sing in A phrygian, and the altos sing in D dorian and D-oriented phrygian. Combined with the use of free chromaticism, these modal touches create a sense of melodic freshness (Example 4.4).

Example 4.4. *Four Madrigals*, "At most mischief," mm. 1-15.

Like its sixteenth-century predecessors, this madrigal also features contrast-ing textures. In m. 25 all four voices sing more homophonically, with a sudden change to a soft dynamic at the words "pitie doth fail in you alas" (Example 4.5).

Example 4.5. *Four Madrigals*, "At most mischief," mm. 21-29.

The fourth madrigal, "Hate whom ye list," while containing sixteenth-century devices, also brings certain twentieth-century techniques to the forefront. In this poem, the lover at first feigns indifference: "Hate and love whom ye list—I care not; do and think what ye wish—I care not." He gives his lady love free rein, but it is apparent that he is very interested in her. In capturing this text in music, Musgrave emphasizes rhythmic vitality, accent, and articulation. The first phrase is set homophonically in an accented, driving rhythm (Example 4.6). In these opening measures, chromaticism is employed to add bite and dissonance to the chords. The

Thea Musgrave

subtle color changes of the harmonies are unpredictable, underscoring the suitor's dubious statements.

Example 4.6. *Four Madrigals*, "Hate whom ye list," mm. 1-11.

Once again, contrasting textures appear at appropriate points in the piece. The *vivo* section "for all is one to me," which is actually a musical quote from the preceding madrigal, resembles an imitative fa-la refrain (Example 4.7).

Thea Musgrave

Example 4.7. *Four Madrigals*, "Hate whom ye list," mm. 61-70.

Although only two melodic ideas are used in this section, the composer maintains interest through tempo, changing meters, metric accents, and dynamic intensity. Musgrave has often acknowledged an appreciation for the music of Monteverdi, and she displays in these earliest choral pieces the same love of contrast and the sorts of dramatic elements evident in the madrigals of Monteverdi's middle period.

> When I had just come back from Paris, I used to work with a group of singers [Saltire Singers]—just four people—and we used to go on tour all around Scotland, so I wrote them that piece. It was written literally for four singers, so the vocal parts don't divide. Many years later the King's Singers asked whether they could adapt it. . . . I heard them do my four madrigals in this version at Carnegie Hall when they came for their American tour; they were really fabulous.[20]

Cantata for a Summer's Day

Another example of Musgrave's early style is *Cantata for a Summer's Day*, which was written for BBC Scotland radio and dedicated to the memory of Lili Boulanger and which she wrote the year after she completed the madrigals. The work is scored for vocal quartet or chamber chorus, speaker, flute, clarinet, and string quintet, including double bass. The part of the reciter and the words of the coda are by Alexander Hume (1550-1609). All other poems are by Maurice Lindsay, friend of the composer and well-known Scottish poet who has collaborated with Musgrave on several works since. In a series of solo and ensemble numbers linked together by short melodramas, the cantata conjures up the sultriness of a Scottish summer's day, from dawn to sunset. Musgrave continues her use of modality combined with a lyric quality, and shows early evidence of her sensitive use of vocal color, which later takes on greater significance.

Movement IVa, "Song of the Burn," has been published separately. In this ode to a stream, the poet Lindsay sets wonderful sounds into motion: the rush and roar of the stream as it goes its way to the river, soft and loud, tumbling and dripping, foaming and flying into the air, and splashing into a pool. The mood is one of joy. Musgrave enhances this buoyant text in several ways. First, the undulating rhythm of an ever-changing pattern of rests propels the "murmell" motive forward. Second, Musgrave displays a Debussyian interest in color (Example 4.8)

116   Thea Musgrave

Example 4.8. "Song of the Burn," mm. 1-10.

At the beginning, Musgrave introduces a gentle, rocking ostinato figure in the tenor and alto voices, as the "stream's waters move head over heels." The ostinato duet then moves to other pairs of voices; throughout, the "murmell" motif is ever present, ever changing. The dark sound of the bass voice is left out until the "tumbling waterfall sings"—a brilliant touch of word-painting. *Four Madrigals* and *Cantata for a Summer's Day* are the only two choral works from Musgrave's early period.

Musgrave did not compose any choral pieces during her serial period. When asked why she had not, she responded:

> It is difficult to write serial music for chorus. Technically it can of course be done, and done without making it extraordinarily difficult (often with almost exclusive emphasis on musical materials that singers don't like to sing). Richard Rodney Bennett has written several works with such ease and fluency.

Serial writing can be regarded as another way of building harmonic and melodic material that relate closely to each other. In a way I think it is a pity that Schoenberg wrote so much about the technical aspects of twelve tone composition because it has led people to think more about the theory than the music. The theory is of course fascinating but should not get in the way of the direct emotional experience music can give.[21]

Musgrave's experience writing atonal music clearly influences her later compositions. The music of the following period represents a departure from her earlier lyric style. Melodic lines are more angular and are fragmented. Musgrave's atonal music freed her from reliance on strict tonal centers. Thus, in the years that followed, she used all twelve tones more freely than before, creating a sense of tonal ambivalence. Her interest in vocal color, already apparent in her earlier compositions, is extended.

"Memento Creatoris"

"Memento Creatoris," Musgrave's first sacred choral piece, is an anthem scored for SAT soloists and SATB choir with optional organ. The text by John Donne advises the listener to remember, while experiencing youth, health, and success, that all is owed to God the Creator—all the riches (means) and lights and even the ability to choose between them. Several different tonal centers, principally C and D^b, are suggested at the beginning of "Memento." In the opening measure of the work, all four voices start on middle C and fan out by half and whole steps. This coloristic effect, which Musgrave repeats several times in varied forms, always underscores the words "remember thy Creator." The dissonant cluster with tonal center on C on the word "Creator" in m. 2 conflicts with tonal center D^b implied by the descending bass line in m. 4 (Example 4.9). This tonal ambiguity is eventually reconciled to A^b by the conclusion of the piece.

Example 4.9. "Memento Creatoris," mm. 1-6.

The melodic lines, though singable, are fragmented and are highly varied rhythmically, as can be seen in Example 4.10. Voices are often paired, and the texture varies from homophonic and heterophonic to contrapuntal.

Example 4.10. "Memento Creatoris," mm. 11-13.

That Musgrave's interest in clarity of text-setting and in text-painting continues can be seen in Example 4.11. A recurring motive of descending sextuplets to the words "made thee of nothing" is enhanced by reducing the choral texture and emerges out of nothing each time it appears, humbling reader, singer, and listener.

　　　　　　　　　　Thea Musgrave

Numerology plays a role in the use of the sextuplet figure, which corresponds to
the number of days that God took to create the world.

　　　Example 4.11. "Memento Creatoris," mm. 35-37.

"John Cook"

"John Cook," Musgrave's shortest choral work, is a product of the same period as
"Memento Creatoris." This part-song for unaccompanied SATB chorus uses an
anonymous text:

> John Cook had a little grey mare;
> Her back stood up and her bones were bare.
> John Cook was riding up Shuter's bank
> And there his nag did kick and prank.
> John Cook was riding up Shuter's Hill
> His mare fell down and made her will.
> The bridle and the saddle were laid on the shelf;
> If you want any more you may make it yourself.

　　　With a short rhythmic ostinato using the intervals of a minor second and a
tritone, Musgrave once again reveals her preference for tonal ambiguity. The ostinato
is transposed each time it recurs and is passed between pairs of voices, a technique
seen in earlier works—"Song of the Burn," for instance. In "John Cook" the texture is thin and sparse: rarely do all four parts sound at the same time. Angular
melodic lines are also found here, highlighted by careful attention to articulation
and dynamic markings (Example 4.12).

Example 4.12. "John Cook," mm. 39-45.

Rorate Coeli

In the 1970s, with her return to opera composition, Musgrave also established a more dramatic style in her choral writing. In general she expanded her compositional palette: vocal color and effects are paramount. She achieves these effects through larger vocal forces and ranges, asynchronous techniques, and more detailed indications of articulation and dynamics. Going beyond the tonally ambivalent and chromatic harmonic language of earlier periods, Musgrave's style is now clearly pantonal.

When asked if it was more difficult for a choir to make use of the dramatic-abstract techniques of the concertos, Musgrave replied:

> I don't see why not so long as it's realized in a practical way. However, I don't usually embark on a piece with any *a priori* formal or technical ideas. Those will be suggested by the poem itself.
>
> I had already chosen the Christmas part of the Dunbar poem, but to this day I remember my excitement when, almost by chance, I happened on the Easter part of the poem and I knew that there had to be a way of meshing the two texts.
>
> Working with the two poems side by side led me to search for an unusual and dramatic form to accommodate them.
>
> The very first musical idea was a simple one: the echoing effect of a single chord shared between full chorus and soloists. This is an important motive for the whole work.
>
> Then I began to make other kinds of divisions: strict tempo along with the free tempo; two different unrelated tempi together; and in another place I indicated what the two soprano soloists should sing but without giving exact pitches—

a kind of improvisation that I thought might appeal to a singer's imagination and sense of adventure! The challenge then in rehearsals is to encourage the performers to do it convincingly *as if* it were all written down. Above all to make it dramatic and soloistic.

I realized then that what I was doing in this work was using some of the technical ideas that I had used in instrumental music.[22]

Rorate Coeli, a brilliant, virtuosic piece, is scored for SSATB soloists and a large SATB choir often divided into eight parts. This piece involves the juxtaposition of two highly descriptive and complicated poems by Scottish poet William Dunbar (1465-1520), both of them written in Middle Scots.[23] The two poems— "Rorate Coeli"and "On the Resurrection of Christ"—make use of recurring Latin phrases. The Latin sentences of "Rorate Coeli," from the liturgy for Christmas Eve and Christmas Day, are verses from Isaiah that prophesy the coming of Christ. The refrain "Surrexit Dominus de sepulcro" in "On the Resurrection of Christ" is a versicle that opens an anonymous hymn used in the Mass for Easter Day according to the Sarum Rite. The nativity poem asks all creation to join in the joyful hymn honoring Christ:

> Sinners be glad, and penance do,
> And thank your maker hairtfully;
> . . . .
> Celestrial fowl in the air
> Sing with your notes upon height
> . . . .
> Now spring up flowers fro' the root,
> Revert you upward naturally,
> . . . .

The companion piece to the nativity poem celebrates the victory represented by the resurrection. This hymn describes the triumph of life over death, spring over winter, and man over himself:

> Done is the battle of dragon black,
> Our campion Christ confoundit had his force;
> . . . .
> The foe is chased, the battle is done cease,
> The prison broken, the jevellouris fleit and flemit;
> . . . .

The rich, sonorous chord to which Musgrave refers in her previous statement is a second-inversion major-minor seventh chord based on E. This chord is first introduced in a broad, unmetered introductory measure by the main chorus in five parts, echoed by a solo ensemble in five parts (Example 4.13).

Example 4.13. *Rorate Coeli*, m. 1.

In measure 3, soloists and seven-part chorus join forces in a full-bodied tutti statement of "Rorate Coeli," before once again echoing one another and fading to a softer dynamic on an E^9 chord to end the introduction. These pillar chords recur in various guises as the piece unfolds and are most clearly recognizable in sections L through N. The chord's most memorable repetition occurs at rehearsal P to the text "sing heaven imperial, sing, make harmony." The same echoing device that opened the work is reintroduced, with the central chord punctuating almost every measure to the end of the piece.

In *Rorate Coeli*, texture and timbre are not ends in themselves; rather, they are geared toward a dramatic and coloristic interpretation of the text. There are as many as twelve different parts sounding simultaneously. The soloists operate as a quintet and as individual soloists. The choral lines are frequently divided, though rarely all at the same time. Where text delineation had been important earlier, here Musgrave subordinates specific words in favor of overall dramatic effect. In Example 4.14 the listener cannot possibly perceive the inner parts, marked *pp sotto voce*, at such a fast tempo and in sesquialtera. Another example of asynchronous writing is given below (Example 4.15), where Musgrave instructs the tenors and altos to sing "ad lib. *not* together. Sing *slowly*, like a tolling bell." In Example 4.16 she achieves a coloristic effect by using tone clusters: while the sopranos and altos sing "any pitch within the range indicated," the basses speak very rapidly at a low pitch and not together the text "Done is the battle of dragon black." Sometimes carefully notated clusters dissolve into improvised clusters, as in Example 4.17.

Example 4.14. *Rorate Coeli*, mm. 7-9.

Example 4.15. *Rorate Coeli*, rehearsal B.

*Ad lib. *not* together. Sing *slowly*, like a tolling bell.

Example 4.16. *Rorate Coeli*, rehearsal D.

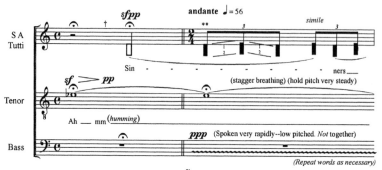

† Sing any pitch within the range indicated
(result should be a closely-spaced cluster)

** Move up and down a semitone from chosen pitch.

Example 4.17. *Rorate Coeli*, rehearsal N.

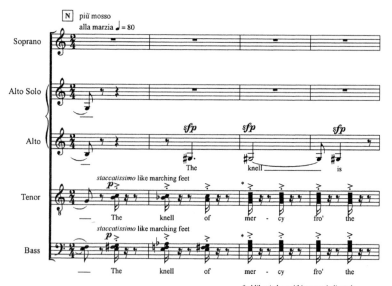

*ad lib. pitches within range indicated;
change pitch on each syllable.

The soloists' parts vary from intoned, recitative-like lines—such as that sung by the bass in Example 4.18, to vocally demanding lines using extreme ranges, such as the imitative duet for the sopranos in Example 4.19. The careful indications of articulation and dynamics in this example are typical of Musgrave's vocal writing at the time, as is the mixture of improvisation and fixed melodic writing.

Example 4.18. *Rorate Coeli*, rehearsal F.

**Dungen = struck down

Example 4.19. *Rorate Coeli*, rehearsal J.

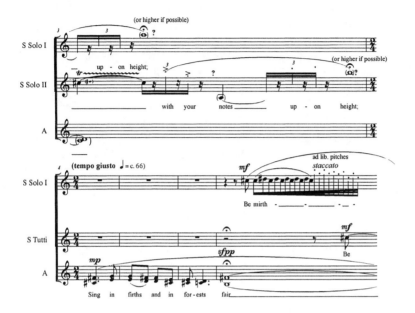

The Last Twilight

The Last Twilight (1980), Musgrave's most extensive choral work since *The Phoenix and the Turtle* (1962) and *Five Ages of Man* (1963), is scored for choir and twelve brass instruments: four horns in F, four trumpets, three tenor trombones, one bass trombone, and a battery of percussion instruments, including solo part for vibraphone. The text, "Men in New Mexico," is a poem written by D. H. Lawrence (1985-1930) in the early 1920s during his three-year stay in Taos, New Mexico. Musgrave was commissioned to write the work by the D. H. Lawrence Festival of New Mexico, which heard its first performance at the Paolo Solieri Theatre in Santa Fe on July 20, 1980.

Although imbued with nature-based metaphors like mountains, desert, and sun, the poem evokes a bleak picture of man's inability to transcend the omnipresence of the landscape or weight of culture and history. Mountains are "blanket-wrapped, they can't wake." These images are compared to the plights of the Native American and the white man, neither of whom are able to wake. In describing the Native Americans, for example, Lawrence incorporates dark, black images to underscore their dilemma and paralysis: "A membrane of sleep, like a black blanket, . . . a dark membrane over the will, . . . born with a caul, a black membrane over the face, and unable to tear it, though the mind is awake." Each group described in the poem longs for something or someone to wake them, but reality shows that these desires are, at best, an illusion. Although "the Indians thought the white man would wake them," even the "white men scramble asleep in the mountains" of America, "And ride on horseback asleep forever through the desert / And shoot one another, amazed and mad with somnambulism / Thinking death will awaken something."

Both white men and Native Americans are under the blanket, stifled, oblivious, asleep, and there is no release from being deprived of movement, fire, and life.[24] Andrew Porter captures the atmosphere in a sentence: "Musgrave's *Last Twilight* is a large, romantic, picturesque evocation of New Mexico's landscape and history, seen in a terrible and beautiful Lawrentian vision."[25] He goes on to comment, "Musgrave's writing for voices and brasses, drums and bells is inspired."[26]

Musgrave divides the large forces into two groups: a main chorus, representing the white man, and a semichorus, representing the Native Americans. Intended as a theatrical piece, *The Last Twilight* also features nonsinging, actors, including supernumeraries (torchbearers), Penitentes who are a religious sect of flagellants from the Sangre de Christos Mountains in New Mexico, and a gunman. Stage directions and lighting are suggested in the score, though a nonstaged version of the work is possible.

Throughout the piece, Musgrave makes effective use of timbre and texture, as well as evocative use of harmony. The opening section of the piece, for example, begins with brass and percussion. The brass sounds in a low, dark octave register and symbolizes the words "blanket-wrapped" and "sleep." These dark colors, combined with hushed dynamics, create a veil of uneasiness, an emotion that will be heightened as the piece progresses (Example 4.20). In measure 6, the Native American semichorus murmurs the word "sleep," *pianissimo.* Although the tonality centers on D, the consistent use of half-steps and tritones conveys a sense of restlessness. The main chorus enters in m. 20 with the main body of the text, and new pitches are added; the octave registration is expanded for increased brilliance. The layering effect of both instrumental and vocal writing is symbolic, again, of the layers of sleep, inertia, and fear. The tessitura of all vocal parts, especially that of the sopranos, lies low.

Example 4.20. *The Last Twilight*, mm. 1-12.

The opening section reappears in the final 46 measures of the piece, representing a circular conception of time in which there is no beginning or end, but just an eternal cycle of paralysis. There is a brief but significant moment of animated word-painting at the line "and though the sun leaps like a thing unleashed in the sky," toward the end of the piece (Example 4.21), but otherwise Musgrave rarely uses sixteenth-note motion.

Thea Musgrave

Example 4.21. *The Last Twilight*, rehearsal 43.

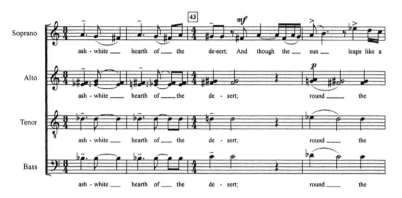

Not even the sun, symbol of ultimate freedom, can release those trapped in their existence. Throughout the work Musgrave increases the number of dissonant intervals and sonorities to underline the disturbing, smoldering paralysis. Pitch clusters are used for purposes of color; tonal centers shift constantly. The piece features various synthetic scales, including octatonic and whole tone, as well as the more traditional harmonic minor scale.

As in earlier pieces, Musgrave borrows material. At rehearsal 26, "Dies Irae" can be heard in the brass as the Penitentes process slowly across the stage. At rehearsal 10, the Native Americans begin a slow ritual dance and sing a theme suggested to Musgrave "by a round dance song by Taos Pueblo from New Mexico."[27] During the ritual dance, the semichorus sings the most highly ornamented passage in the piece, a heterophonically conceived texture reminiscent of Native American music (Example 4.22).

Example 4.22. *The Last Twilight*, mm. 57-66.

*Theme suggested by a round dance song by Taos Pueblo, New Mexico; the words are the composer's own.

Lesser Works

For "O caro m'è il sonno" (1974), a very short unaccompanied madrigal for STB soloists and mixed choir, Musgrave returns to the style of text and music seen in her *Four Madrigals*. The Italian text of the poem, by Renaissance painter Michelangelo Buonarroti (1475-1564), is given in Appendix M.

O how dear to me is sleep—
it is more the likeness of stone.
While the harm and the shame lasts,
not to see, not to hear
is for me a great fortune.
For that reason don't disturb me,
rather speak softly.

In this piece Musgrave returns to her earlier, lyric style and creates a contemporary Italian madrigal, yet her approach differs from that in the English madrigals written more than twenty years before. The melodic lines are marked *espressivo* and are lyric, yet they are also extremely chromatic. Like Gesualdo, Musgrave uses chromaticism and dissonance for dramatic effect. In the text, the poet yearns for oblivion, stone-like sleep. Musgrave pictures this yearning by leaving suspensions or tendency tones unresolved; the piece has not one moment of rest nor a single cadence. Musgrave takes care to mark each note with precise articulation and desired dynamics. The first eight measures of this twenty-four-measure piece show the care, economy, and expressiveness of Musgrave's writing (Example 4.23).

Example 4.23. "O caro m'è il sonno," mm. 1-8.

In a more recent choral composition, "The Lord's Prayer" (1984) for chorus and organ, Musgrave returns to a traditional presentation of the text. Cluster harmonies and coloristic effects in the organ contrast with the tertian-based harmonies heard in the choral parts, which Musgrave presents in a straightforward manner in this tightly organized piece. Melodic lines are reminiscent of her earlier lyric style. Musgrave achieves unity through use of a recurring descending half-step E♭ to D (sometimes expanded to a whole step, E♭ to D♭), which changes registers in the organ as the work progresses. This octave displacement creates a sense of movement through the piece. The half-step or whole-step motif recurs often in the organ, and references to it in the choral parts are clearly apparent (see Example 4.24).

Example 4.24. "The Lord's Prayer," mm. 32-35 and mm. 50-56.

Thus in "The Lord's Prayer" Musgrave combines techniques typical of her most recent compositional style with devices she has used throughout her career.

In 1986 Musgrave completed *Black Tambourine* for women's chorus, piano, and six percussion parts to be performed by singers in the chorus. The seventeen-minute work is in six sections and uses poems from Hart Crane's last collection, *White Buildings*. *Black Tambourine* is an accessible work, more traditional than her recent, more asynchronous scores.

For the Time Being (1987), commissioned by the BBC Singers, is Musgrave's longest unaccompanied choral work. The poem of the same name by W. H. Auden was published in 1945. Subtitled "A Christmas Oratorio," it was written with the wish, never fulfilled, that it be set to music by Benjamin Britten. *For the Time Being* is divided into five continuous movements that follow the layout of the poem. Musgrave uses some of Auden's "chorus," "semichorus," "narrator," and "recitative" subdivisions.[28]

Echoes Through Time (1988) was commissioned by Agnes Scott College and is a staged dramatic piece for SA chorus and five solo voices, five spoken roles, small chamber orchestra, and an optional set of three dancers.[29]

The texts for Musgrave's three unaccompanied sets of choral works called "Poems on the Underground" are drawn from a book, *Poems on the Underground,* by Gerald Benson, Judith Chernik, and Cecily Herbert. In Set I, "On gratitude, love and madness," six short, carefully chosen, unified poems are set for SATB chorus with ample divisi. Poems about gratitude frame the set of six, James Berry's "Benediction" opens and "Sometimes" by Sheenagh Pugh closes. The middle settings balance humor ("Lady Singleton" by Stevie Smith), character portraits (Adrienne Rich's "Aunt Jennifer"), love (W. B. Yeats's "Her Anxiety"), and madness ("Much Madness is divinest Sense" by Emily Dickinson).

Set II, "The Strange and the Exotic," encompasses three poems. Two musical settings of Robert Herricks's "Dreams" frame two images of peacocks and piranhas (poems by seventeenth-century anonymous and Edwin Morgan respectively). "The Subway Piranhas," a poem commissioned for the inauguration of the refurbished Glasgow's underground, was not presented there but had to wait for Musgrave to set it musically. Musically economical and without divisi, this set is short, colorful, and accessible.

"A Medieval Summer," Set III, for SATB chorus with frequent divisi, solo soprano, alto, and tenor uses several staging devices reminiscent of earlier instrumental works. The music, intended as a musical tapestry of medieval times, engages an offstage tenor to portray the betrayer of love, the Cuckoo, in the famous thirteenth-century round *Sumer is icumen in, loude sing cockoo.* Illustrations are given to map the chorus placement and movement of the soloists.

Wild Winter was commissioned by the Lichfield Festival to commemorate the city's Civil War siege. The work takes its title from a Wilfred Owen work and is scored for SATB chorus, soprano solo, and viol consort. The extended piece (nineteen minutes) interweaves poems and musical responses that describe the universal horrors of war. Poetic excerpts are taken from Federico García Lorca (in Spanish), Stephen Crane (in English), Victor Hugo (in French), Aleksandr Sergeevich Pushkin (in Russian), Francesco Petrarca (in Italian), and Georg Trakl (in German).

When asked what her music is like, Musgrave replied:

To me composition is just an incredible adventure. I hope my music is dramatic, that it is accessible if given a little time to get to the listener, that it has warmth, perhaps a certain amount of humor, some comedy elements—rather than saying I am a serial or romantic composer. I use many elements of music, even some aleatoric passages, and try to draw them all together. I hope I have a style that is recognizable and individual.[30]

Notes

1. William Bender, "The Musgrave Ritual—Romancing the Woman Who Wasn't There," *Time*, October 10, 1977, 72.
2. Thea Musgrave quoted in Donald L. Hixon, *Thea Musgrave—A Bio-Bibliography* (Westport, CT: Greenwood Press, 1984), 3.
3. Thea Musgrave quoted in Hixon, *Thea Musgrave—A Bio-Bibliography*, 3.
4. Allen Sapp, "Thea Musgrave: A Perspective," unpublished paper delivered Thursday, January 16, 1986, at the College-Conservatory of Music, University of Cincinnati.
5. Andrew Porter, "Some New British Composers," *Musical Quarterly* 51 (1969-1970): 57.
6. *The New Grove Dictionary of Music and Musicians*, s.v. "Thea Musgrave," by Stephen Walsh.
7. Thea Musgrave quoted in David Ewen, ed. and comp., *Composers Since 1900: A Biographical and Critical Guide*, First Supplement (New York: H. W. Wilson and Co., 1981), 203.
8. Thea Musgrave, "Starting Points," *The Listener* 81 (1969): 153.
9. Amalia Elguera, "The Birth of Ariadne," *The Listener* 13 (June 1974): 769.
10. Thea Musgrave quoted in Shirley Fleming, "Thea Musgrave's Elusive 'Ariadne,'" *New York Times*, September 25, 1977, 19.
11. Andrew Porter, "Thea Musgrave's *Voice of Ariadne*," *New Yorker*, October 24, 1977, 164.
12. Christopher Ford, "Double Concerto," *Guardian* (Manchester, England), August 9, 1973, 9.
13. Andrew Porter, "Mary," *New Yorker*, May 1, 1978, 136.
14. Annalyn Swan, "Carol," *Newsweek*, December 17, 1979, 88.
15. Patrick J. Smith, "Harriet, the Women Called Moses—Thea Musgrave's New Success," *Opera* 36 (May 1985): 493.
16. Nadia Boulanger was the first woman to conduct the Philadelphia Orchestra; Elaine Brown, founder and director of Singing City from 1949 to 1989, was the second.
17. Thea Musgrave quoted in Hixon, *Thea Musgrave—A Bio-Bibliography*, 7.
18. Interview with Thea Musgrave by the author, College-Conservatory of Music, Cincinnati, Ohio, January 16, 1986.
19. Appendix J contains a complete listing, in chronological order, of Musgrave's choral compositions.
20. Interview with Thea Musgrave, January 15, 1986.
21. Interview with Thea Musgrave, January 15, 1986. (In the quote Musgrave is referring to *Variations for Orchestra*, Opus 31, by Arnold Schoenberg.)

22. Interview with Thea Musgrave, January 15, 1986.
23. See Appendix K for the complete text of *Rorate Coeli.*
24. Appendix L contains the complete text of "Men in New Mexico" by D. H. Lawrence.
25. Andrew Porter, "Reviews," *New Yorker*, March 29, 1982, 133.
26. Porter, "Reviews," *New Yorker*, 133.
27. Cited in Thea Musgrave, *The Last Twilight*, piano-vocal score (Borough Green, England: Novello, 1981), 12.
28. See *A Descriptive Analysis of Two Recent Choral Works by Thea Musgrave:* Black Tambourine *and* For The Time Being: Advent, by Laura Louise Lane. D.M.A. Essay, University of Iowa, May 1989.
29. Scored for: flute, piccolo, oboe, 2 clarinets, bassoon, violin, piano doubling synthesizer, harp, timpani doubling percussion, percussion, and strings. Prerecorded optional prologue and epilogue to be played in lobbies and halls.
30. Thea Musgrave quoted in Hans Heinsheimer, "Mistress Musgrave," *Opera News* 42 (September 1977): 44-45.

The Contemporary Period

Other Voices, Old and New

Recent literature pertaining to the English Musical Renaissance continues to ignore, almost entirely, the substantial choral contributions of Lutyens, Maconchy, and Musgrave, as well as more contemporary composers such as Nicola LeFanu or Judith Weir. In *British Choral Music: A Millennium Performing Conspectus of Nineteenth & Twentieth Century Music for Choral Societies,* edited by Lewis Foreman in 2001, none of these women composers are recognized. Indeed, only three merit a notation in the select list, and none of them were chosen for performance during the centennial year. The author's introductory comments attempt to explain the reason (but are illustrative of yet another cause for concern) and fail to capture the inherent contradiction in the succeeding paragraph of the introductory chapter:

> Overall—and I speak with 40 years practical experience—my feeling was reinforced that at the end of the day the man (unfortunately we were presented with no women conductors) out front is responsible for what ensures.
>   . . . In my view generally choral repertoire is chosen from a limited list of long-standing favorites, which is why a competition to present revivals was such a good idea. Eventually we become damaged by repetition and ultimately it becomes boring only to do the things that are loved.[1]

The authors of this tiny volume present a repertoire list whose "function was not prescriptive but to suggest works and composers worth exploring."[2] Ruth Gipps' (1921-1999) *The Cat* is listed, as is *The Golden Threshold* by Liza Lehmann (1862-1918), and not surprisingly Ethel Smyth's (1858-1944) *The Prison.*

The controversy and frequently dissonant discussion regarding the content of *The Musical Renaissance 1840-1940: Constructing a National Music* is not really relevant here. For this, the most recent book (revised in 2001) makes scant mention of any women composers.

The Music Makers: The English Musical Renaissance from Elgar to Britten[3] makes no mention of the Macnaghten-Lemare Concerts, nor are there any entries in the index under the names of Lutyens, Maconchy, or Musgrave. This invisibility is a blessing, perhaps, considering the treatment given Dame Ethel Smyth in the same book:

> It is as a character and a celebrated sapphist that she is likely to continue to be best known in the future, for her music—the chief interest of her life—has gone into almost total eclipse, and there are no grounds for believing that this position will or should be reversed. While she was alive and promoting her own works Smyth's music received performance and attention. After her death, in 1944, however, the musical works slipped from sight; some would say deservedly so. . . . As a woman, however, she will doubtless never cease to be of interest.[4]

The Macnaghten-Lemare Concerts, so important in 1931 when they were founded, continued until 2000. Maconchy notes:

> Myself and a number of others had our first works played—and so have young composers ever since, and still do to the present day. It was probably the best thing that ever happened for young composers here, and it was the only thing that happened for a long time.[5]

Thus the generation of Elisabeth Lutyens, Elizabeth Maconchy, Grace Williams, Priaulx Rainier, Imogen Holst, Elizabeth Poston, Phyllis Tate, and Dorothy Gow paved the way for following generations. According to Maconchy:

> When I was young there were half a dozen women composers of about the same age in England, though not I think elsewhere. This was something new, previously there had been the isolated figure of Ethel Smyth, and since then there have been very few new composers, with the notable exception of Thea Musgrave. Is it the impresarios and powers-that-be who keep the gateway to success? Yes—I think it is. Now forty years after my generation, another group of young women has come on the scene: Gillian Whitehead, Anna Lockwood, Jennifer Fowler, Melanie Daiken, Helen Longworth, Erika Fox, Margaret Lucy Wilkins, Nicola LeFanu to name only some of them. Nicola LeFanu is my daughter, and this gives me a particular interest in what the younger generation is doing and is a personal link with them through her and her friends, which I value very much.[6]

In the 1960s and early 1970s the musical climate of England was very favorable, and real opportunity existed for young women receiving a musical education. During these years, London was considered a great center of contemporary music. For Lutyens, Maconchy, and Musgrave, this was a time for numerous commissions and for frequent performances and programming of their works. Stravinsky wrote:

> The open-door policy to new music in England in the last few years was made possible to a large extent by the accession of an intelligent younger generation in the musical press. In consequence, London has become a great capital of contemporary music.[7]

Andrew Porter continues:

> The whole thing snowballed. . . . It was a little thrill, a little unnatural. The old guard—and not only the old guard—were dismayed when *The Times*, formerly a repository of accepted opinion, cried that we should hear less Beethoven, more Berio, or, after *Sul ponte de Hiroshima*, that Luigi Nono was the Verdi of our day.[8]

It was in these days that Nicola LeFanu, the daughter of Elizabeth Maconchy, was attending the Royal College of Music. Unfortunately, soon after she had begun to be noticed as a composer, the kind of encouragement her mother had finally felt was no longer forthcoming. She writes:

> I grew up secure in the belief that discrimination against women in music, such as had beset my mother's generation, was a thing of the past. I began my career in a city that was called the musical capital of the world, and I was intoxicated by the diversity of opportunities, by the marvelous range of concerts. I could never have imagined for a moment the effects of the oligarchy of the 1980s. I came to London's concert halls as a young woman and heard The Fires of London playing Gillian Whitehead, the Allegri Quartet playing Jennifer Fowler, Jane Manning singing Erika Fox, the CBSO playing a new orchestral work of mine. . . . I believed, in my naivety, that this was the beginning of the good times: that all that Elisabeth Lutyens, Priaulx Rainier, my mother Elizabeth Maconchy and the other women composers in that generation had stood for and struggled for was finally bearing fruit. In 1973 I had an orchestral commission for the BBC Promenade Concerts; there were four commissions that year, and three went to women (the other two were Thea Musgrave and Rainier). In the same year I went to the United States on a Harkness Fellowship, and there I came across musicians in the Women's Movement for the first time. I was very smug when asked if anyone had yet started a Women in Music in England. Oh yes, I said, someone had started the Society for Women Musicians in 1912, and it had just closed down with a triumphant diamond jubilee concert celebrating the achievement of its aims.[9]

Confident—even smug—as she was, LeFanu was soon to learn with striking clarity that the bright future for women that her mother's generation had dreamed had not materialized. LeFanu notes in 1988 that the decline in support for women composers is evident from the following statistics: although women composers number about 15 percent of the working composers in Britain, out of a total of forty commissions given over a fourteen-year period (1973-1987), the Proms awarded only one to a woman. Disbursements from major grants organizations for commissions and tours of new works by women fell to just 6 percent of all applications between 1972 and 1986. LeFanu's research also revealed that significant music festivals held in 1986 and 1987 programmed little or no music by women composers. LeFanu demonstrates her argument about women's increasing invisibility by citing Paul Griffiths' book, *New Sounds, New Personalities: British Composers of the 1980s*, which includes twenty contemporary composers. Not one composer is a woman!

Nicola LeFanu mentioned recently that the article quoted above, and various broadcasts on the same theme, have had amazing repercussions. The alarming statistics presented in the article have caused people to reexamine the challenge to women composers writing in the 1980s.[10]

In spite of some noticeable strides in performance time for compositions by women composers over the last twenty years, support for commissions and contemporary music performance reflects the diminished funding for the arts in general. Periodically, hopeful but rare trends appear. In August 2003, three works by living female composers Judith Weir, Sally Beamish, and American Libby Larson, all English premieres, were performed at the BBC Proms. At the end of her article "Great mistresses: Annette Morreau on three women taking the baton in another male-dominated world (women II)," Morreau concludes:

> The problem for female composers seems to be not one of talent, but of access. Lack of access breeds lack of confidence. If the opportunities for performance— the Proms, for instance—are so tiny, the pressure to succeed is tremendous. If there were a female controller of music for BBC Radio 3, or a female composer laureate, might the pressures be different?[11]

An unusual number of significant English composers were born in the first decade of the twentieth century: Priaulx Rainier, 1903-1987; Elizabeth Poston, 1905-1987; Grace Williams, 1906-1977; Elisabeth Lutyens, 1906-1983; Imogen Holst, 1907-1984; Elizabeth Maconchy, 1907-1994. Their sheer numbers and their tenacity created a wave that still is felt. The forward motion has been interrupted by a backlash revealed by Nicola LeFanu in "Master Musician: An Impregnable Taboo?" However, the force of their musical and organizational accomplishments is far-reaching and undeniable.

Phyllis Tate

Phyllis Tate (1911-1987), a contemporary of Lutyens and Maconchy, contributed distinguished choral compositions to the repertoire. She studied with Harry Farjeon at the Royal Academy of Music and was a fellow there in 1964. Tate is not a prolific composer, but choral works, all published by Oxford University Press, occupy a central core of her output. There are eight extended works for chorus that sometimes include unusual and colorful instrumental combinations, such as *Seven Lincolnshire Folk Songs* (1966), for two-part choir, percussion (two players), piano (four hands), celeste, and double bass. Tate also wrote *A Secular Requiem* (1967) for choir, woodwind, brass, and—unexpectedly—four cellos. For the requiem she set "The Phoenix and the Turtle," a text attributed to Shakespeare, which Thea Musgrave also set for chorus and orchestra five years earlier. *St. Martha and the Dragon* (1976) is scored for soloists, chorus, and chamber orchestra of oboe, horn, harp, piano, harmonium, organ, guitar, timpani, percussion, strings, and tape. A number of short choral works are published, including pieces for unaccompanied mixed chorus and several selections for women's voices. Tate is also known for two-part choral songs. "She is aware of a need to communicate with a wide public, and her children's music stems naturally from her other creative work."[12]

Grace Williams

Grace Williams (1906-1977), a Welsh composer, studied in Cardiff before moving to London to continue her studies with Vaughan Williams at the Royal College of Music. She was the most prolific choral composer of those mentioned, with many works published and other works available in manuscript. The choral output of Grace Williams, not unlike that of her lifelong friend Maconchy, did not begin to appear until late in her life. Outstanding among her secular works are *All Seasons Shall Be Sweet* (1963), a set of nine choral pieces, scored for soprano solo, women's chorus (SSA), piano, and orchestra; *Carmina avium* (1967), for mixed chorus, viola d'amore, viola, and harp; and a very approachable choral work, her only work for male choir—except for a much earlier work, *Ye Highlands and Ye Lowlands*, written in 1972 for TTBB and piano. Sacred music occupies a relatively small part of Grace Williams' output. Her setting of "Ave Maris Stella" ("Hail Star of the Sea," 1973) for unaccompanied SATB chorus, one of the best known Latin hymns to the Virgin, is perhaps her most impressive work. The first three words of the hymn form a refrain that opens every stanza, and the plastic rhythms reflect the ebb and flow of the sea, as do the undulating melodic lines and the skillful changes in vocal color. *Missa Cambrensis* (1971), her last large-scale work, is scored for SATB chorus, boys' choir, and orchestra; incorporates nonliturgical material into the Latin rite; and uses sections of text from the Welsh Bible, words from a Welsh Christmas carol by Saunders Lewis, and segments from the Latin rite. The sound of bells, the use of a distant boys' choir, and the interval of the tritone color the score, and the work as a whole shows the influence of the Britten *War Requiem*.

Up to now (1980) the *Missa Cambrensis* has been heard only once, in a performance which did nothing to minimize the formidable challenge it presents, above all to the choral singers. It may not be an unflawed masterpiece, but it is a work of great power, rich in incident, generous in feeling, and exemplary in craftsmanship. Its continued neglect is something that ought to prick the consciences of all Welsh choral societies.[13]

Priaulx Rainier

Priaulx Rainier (1903-1986), born and raised in South Africa of English-Huguenot parents, went to study at the Royal Academy of Music in 1920. Later, she studied for a short time with Nadia Boulanger and taught composition at the RAM from 1943 to 1961. Rainier's only choral work, a powerful and prophetic *Requiem* (1955), is scored for unaccompanied chorus and tenor solo. The work, recently revived by the BBC Singers in June 1987, was written for Imogen Holst and the BBC Singers. The text, by David Gascoyne, is a warning for prospective victims, a requiem for the ideals and hopes of the world. Rainier's choral writing is homophonic and stark in its rhythmic strength. The incantatory tenor solo acts at times as an integral part of the chorus, while at other times it provides a connection between choral sections and dramatic recitative. At the time Rainier composed the work she wrote:

> Most composed requiems are for the departed, while one or two, such as that by Brahms, are for the survivors. David Gascoyne's poem is for neither: it is for the prospective victims. When writing it, he used words especially suitable for singing and for setting to music; moreover he designed a structure for the music, his verses being designated alternately "voice" and "chorus." . . . I contemplated it throughout the war and indeed for fifteen years before I felt my ideas had sufficiently matured to attempt a setting. It's an essentially mystical text, which . . . could be interpreted as a requiem for the ideals and hopes of the world, and an appeal to the unknown mysterious force for guidance and strength.[14]

Like Maconchy and Lutyens, Rainier, after years of neglect, finally gained recognition and a growing number of commissions in the 1960s, and continued to do so up to the time of her death.

Nicola LeFanu

Nicola LeFanu (1947-) grew up with the sounds of music around her and realized her true vocation while she was still quite young. She read music at Oxford University and studied composition at Harvard University and Brandeis University with Earl Kim and Seymour Shifrin while in the United States on a Harkness

Fellowship. LeFanu, like her mother before her, is actively involved in organizations that promote new music. Currently, she is a music professor at York University. She was the impetus and co-organizer of "Music and Gender," a conference held at King's College, London in the summer of 1991. In a panel discussion during the conference, LeFanu spoke emphatically about the need for compositions by women to be analyzed. These commentaries must be published in the important music journals because such scholarship influences musicologists to take the music more seriously.

LeFanu's choral works include "Christ Calls Man Home" (1971) for SATB unaccompanied choir; "The Valleys Shall Sing" (1973) for SATB chorus, two bassoons, two trumpets, and three trombones; "The Little Valleys" (1975) for female or boys' voices, SSSS (unaccompanied); "Verses from Psalm 90" (1978) for soprano and two mixed choirs, . . . *for we are the stars* (1978) for sixteen singers, arranged in four SATB choirs; *Like a Wave of the Sea* (1981) for mixed choir and ensemble of early instruments; and *Stranded on My Heart* (1984) for tenor solo, SATB chorus, and strings. Recent short unaccompanied works are "The Spirit Moves" (1992) and "On the Wind" (1997).

. . . *for we are the stars* is a colorful and highly evocative work in which LeFanu combines Native American words and sounds with an English translation of her text. Wide leaps characterize the sung lines, and LeFanu attempts to notate some of the native sounds as microtonal glissandos. The work opens with a unison C^4, accented and *forte*, and from the four tenors, who sing a Native American word, "Yallaneya." Seven different pitches sound (with doublings) in m. 3, encompassing over two octaves; in m. 5, the remaining pitches are heard. In m. 7 all voices return to the unison C^4, which awakens and alerts the listener to her sensitive setting of the text. The vast spaces of the universe are conveyed in vocal registration and texture, and the words "stars," "light," "sky," "soul" are etched with ingenuity. The piece portrays in sounds the path of a soul through limitless space in its journey through death. At the climax of the written text (on the word "death"—*molto crescendo, fff*) LeFanu creates a sense of boundless space through which the soul travels. The tempo slows, and all sense of time is distorted as the sopranos and altos, almost imperceptibly, begin singing in sustained half-note motion, creating a universe of space. Textural segments are repeated as the pillar chords return in separate choirs, and several measures from the end of the piece the unison C^4 is heard again.

Judith Weir

Judith Weir (1954-) has contributed significant works to the choral repertoire. She receives a steady stream of commissions and her publishers, Novello and Chester, are committed to promoting her latest compositions.

For someone who states she has little or no background in choral music, Weir has well over fifteen choral works in her catalog.

> I was brought up in the Church of Scotland, where we did sing hymns, but that was really all. I did go and hear the choir [at Kings College Cambridge], but of course I wasn't really part of that world. I approached writing for voices from a certain position of unfamiliarity; it's something I devised for myself.[15]

Judith Weir has studied composition with John Tavener in London and has studied computer music with Barry Vercoe at the Massachusetts Institute of Technology. The catalog of publicly performed works by Judith Weir begins in 1972, and until her extremely successful opera *A Night at the Chinese Opera*, most of her compositions were for small forces, and almost half of them used voice. Her earliest successful choral works include an anthem, *Ascending into Heaven*, for SATB choir and organ; "Illuminare, Jerusalem—Jerusalem rejos for joy," a carol for SATB choir and organ; and *Missa del Cid*. Known for clarity, economy of musical gesture, and wit, Weir has received a number of choral commissions since the late 1990s, especially notable are "Two Human Hymns" (chorus and organ) and *We Are Shadows* for SATB chorus, children's chorus, and orchestra, and "Sanctus," written as part of the *Requiem of Reconciliation*, for SATB chorus and orchestra.

In *Missa del Cid* (1988), written for television, Weir chose portions of the epic poem about El Cid, the eleventh-century Spanish hero, because, she explained: "I couldn't believe the coincidences in the use of language between the poem and the words of the mass, so I decided to write a mass using as my text episodes from the life of the Cid."[16] She intersperses portions of the romanesque poem with fragments of the text from the traditional movements of the Mass. Finally she adds a spoken narration for an Evangelist ("my tribute to TV's invention of the voice-over,"[17] concedes Weir). The work is set for ten unaccompanied voices using a mixture of liturgical Latin, medieval Spanish, and simultaneous English translation of the *El Cid* text.

Summary

Many areas for further research are apparent from the preceding pages. Scholarly articles have yet to be written on the history of the Society of Women Musicians or the Macnaghten-Lemare Concerts. A comparative study of twentieth-century requiems that use nonliturgical texts might include the lesser known works of Lutyens' *Requiem for the Living*, Rainier's *Requiem*, and Tate's *A Secular Requiem*, alongside Britten's better-known *War Requiem* and Hindemith's *When Lilacs Last in the Door-yard Bloom'd*. A study of recent settings of the Mass could well include Weir's *Missa del Cid* and Williams' *Missa Cambrensis*, which combine texts from the Latin rite and other sources. Maconchy, Musgrave, Tate, Weir, and LeFanu have all written noteworthy works for children—pieces that engage young singers in well-written music with drama. These include Musgrave's *Marko the Miser*, Maconchy's *Fly-By-Nights* and *The Birds*, Tate's *St. Martha and the Dragon*, and LeFanu's *The Green Children*.[18] No extended studies have been done on the substantial choral output of either Grace Williams or Phyllis Tate.

The significant number of choral works written by women composers deserves attention through further investigation and performance. In particular, the choral works of Elisabeth Lutyens, Elizabeth Maconchy, and Thea Musgrave merit attention by choral directors and singers alike in the States, so that the American concert repertoire may be enriched and made more diverse.

Notes

1. Lewis Foreman, ed. *British Choral Music: A Millennium Performing Conspectus of Nineteenth & Twentieth Century Music for Choral Societies* (Upminster: British Music Society, 2001), 12.

2. Foreman, *British Choral Music*, 106.

3. Michael Trend, *The Music Makers: The English Musical Renaissance from Elgar to Britten* (London: Weidenfeld and Nicolson, 1985).

4. Trend, *The Music Makers*, 93-94. In light of Trend's observation, it may interest the reader that several recordings have been issued of recent performances of the music of Dame Ethel Smyth. A BBC Philharmonic performance of her opera *The Wreckers* was scheduled for the first broadcast performance ever in 1994, under the direction of Odaline de la Martinez.

5. Elizabeth Maconchy, "A Composer Speaks," *Composer* 42 (Winter 1971-1972): 25.

6. Maconchy, "A Composer Speaks," 29.

7. Igor Stravinsky, *Expositions and Developments*, quoted in Andrew Porter, "Some New British Composers," *Contemporary Music in Europe* (New York: G. Schirmer, 1965), 14.

8. Porter, "Some New British Composers," 14.

9. Nicola LeFanu, "Master Musician: An Impregnable Taboo?" *Contact* 31 (Autumn 1987): 4-8.

10. Letter from Nicola LeFanu to Catherine Roma, December 27, 1988. In fact, at the beginning of November 1987, the Labour Party focused attention on the underrepresentation of women in the arts and media, devoting question time in the House of Commons to it on November 2, and produced a document, "The Missing Culture." The music statistics were based on LeFanu's research for "Master Musician: An Impregnable Taboo?" For more information and articles, see

Women in Music Newsletter 2 (January 1988): 8-9.

11. Annette Morreau, "Great Mistresses: Annette Morreau on three women taking the baton in another male-dominated world. (women II)," *New Statesman, Ltd.*, August 25, 2003.

12. *The New Grove Dictionary of Music and Musicians*, s.v. "Phyllis Tate," by Richard Cooke.

13. Malcolm Boyd, *Grace Williams* (Composers of Wales no. 4, Cardiff: University of Wales Press, 1980), 65.

14. Priaulx Rainier, from a program note written for the BBC Singers Concert, June 5, 1987.

15. Judith Weir, quoted in James Weeks, "Unique Detachment" *Choir and Organ* 12 (March/April 2004), 35.

16. Judith Weir, "Weird World," *Radio Times*, November 26-December 2, 1988, 22.

17. Judith Weir, from the introduction that precedes the performance of BBC-TV 4 broadcast of *Missa del Cid*.

18. Grace Williams has a wealth of well-written choral music for children's voices.

Appendix A

Lutyens' Proposal for the Composer's Concourse

The spelling and punctuation has been left as in the original.

It was in 1953 that I first conceived the idea of trying to create an occasion or a platform for composers to meet and discuss their technical problems and discover what each other was writing. I thought this might be stimulating, and an easing of the state of isolation a composer generally lives and works in. In Paris, where I had been a student, there is the cafe life, centred in one district, when night and day the artists meet and discuss. The London "pubs", in some sort, fulfil this need—(pocket and stomach being willing) but London is too large and unfocussed, and I felt that a more definite and formal platform was, perhaps, called for.

It "sounded" two of my colleagues, Arnold Cooke and Alan Bush, who responded to the idea and we decided to make a start to see how things developed. A provisional Committee was formed consisting of John Amis, Lennox Berkeley, Alan Bush, Ernest Chapman, Arnold Cooke, Eileen Ralf and myself. We each put something in the "kitty" for the cost of the necessary circulation, which was refunded at the end of the first series of talks. Since then the Concourse has run on its own steam.

The Musicians' Benevolent Fund let us have their room at Carlos Place for the meetings, the attendance at which has been between 30 to 50 an evening. Our membership is for people professionally connected with music, or students, though members of the public are admitted and we try to cover all schools of musical thought.

We have planned two or three series of talks during the year, each talk followed by a discussion. We have also taken the opportunity of visits to this country of distinguished musicians to ask them to speak for us i. e. Aaron Copland, Henry Cowell, Aram Khatchaturyan and Sir Eugene Goosens. Two of our talks have been taken by the BBC,—Peter Pears "On Writing for the Voice" and Dr. R. Vaughan Williams on "The Teaching of Sanford". Our series of talks has been:

Theory, Technique and Style in Twentieth Century Music
The Instrumentalist and the Composer
The Composer at Work
Opera and the British Composer
Commissioned Music (The films—radio)
Music and Aesthetics
The Teaching of Musical Composition
Nationalism and the Modern Scene

(I would like to draw particular attention to the series Music and Aesthetics, introduced by Dr. Ruth Saw, B. A., Ph.D., as being the first of its kind in this country.)
The following have taken part in the Concourse as speakers and chairmen.

John Addison	John Denison
Dr. Edward Allam	Lady Fermoy
William Alwyn	Gerald Finzi
Malcolm Arnold	Peter Racine Fricker
Denis ApIvor	William Glock
Lennox Berkeley	Scott Goddard
James Blades	Reginald Goodall
Sir Arthur Bliss	Christopher Hassall
Alan Bush	J. P. Hodin
John Cage	Imogen Holst
Archie Camden	Andree Howard
Edward Clark	Frank Howes
Arnold Cooke	Daniel Jones
John Lambert	Alfred Rodrigues
A. L. Lloyd	Dr. Ruth Saw
Elisabeth Lutyens	Humphrey Searle
Elizabeth Maconchy	Matyas Seiber
Colin Mason	Evan Senior
Wilfred Mellers	R. D. Smith
Frank Merrick	Bernard Stevens
Donald Mitchell	Lionel Tertis
Angus Morrison	Terence Tiller
Oliver Neighbour	Michael Tippett
Bernard Naylor	David Webster
Peter Pears	Eric Walter White
Thomas Pitfield	Dr. R. Vaughan Williams
Alan Rawsthorne	Sir Steuart Wilson
Hans Redlich	Geoffrey Winters
	Basil Wright

The Constitution of the Concourse was submitted by the Committee and ratified at the last Annual General Meeting in June, 1955.

The present Committee is as follows:

John Addison (Vice-Chairman)   William Glock

Alan Bush (Chairman)   Elisabeth Lutyens (Founder)

Arnold Cooke (Hon. Treasurer)

Joyce Rathbone   Christopher Shaw

Miss Kathleen Scarr (Hon. Secretary)

Appendix B

The Published Choral Compositions of Elisabeth Lutyens in Chronological Order

1953
Excerpta Tractati Logico-Philosophici, Op. 27 (10') Motet for unaccompanied SATB chorus. Text: Wittgenstein. Schott

1957
De Amore Op. 39 (40') Cantata for soprano and tenor soli, SATB chorus, orchestra. Text: Chaucer. Schott

1957/1963
Country of the Stars (10') Motet for unaccompanied SATB chorus. Text: Boethius, trans. Chaucer. Novello

1963
Encomion Op. 54 (17') "Let Us Now Praise Famous Men . . ." for SATB chorus, brass, percussion. Text: Sirach from Ecclesiasticus. Schott

1964-5/1970
Hymn of Man Op. 61/Op.61a (10') Hymn for unaccompanied male chorus/mixed chorus. Text: Swinburne. Schott

1965
Magnificat and Nunc Dimittis (10') Motets for unaccompanied SATB chorus. Schott

1968
Essence of Our Happinesses Op. 69 (16') for tenor, SATB chorus, orchestra. Text: Abu Yasid, Donne, Rimbaud. Olivan
The Tyme Doth Flete Op. 70 (19') for unaccompanied SATB chorus. Optional prelude and postlude for four brass. Text: Petrarch, trans. Wyatt/Ovid. Olivan

1970
Verses of Love (8') for unaccompanied SATB chorus. Text: Ben Jonson. Novello

1972
Voice of Quiet Waters Op. 84 (16') for SATB chorus, orchestra. Text: Conrad, Palmer, Wordsworth. Olivan
Counting Your Steps Op. 85 (16') for SATB chorus, four flutes, four percussionists. Text: Pygmy poetry. Olivan

1976
"It Is the Hour" Op. 111a (5') for unaccompanied SATB chorus. Text: Byron. Olivan

1979
Roots of the World Op. 136 (11' 30") for SATB chorus, cello obbligato. Text: W. B. Yeats. Olivan

Appendix C

Withdrawn Choral Works by Elisabeth Lutyens in the British Museum

Accompanied Choral Works

Winter the Huntsman. Set of songs for SATB chorus, trumpet, horn, cello, double bass, and piano

Electra. For two SATB choruses and piano

"Kibbutznik's Song." For SATB chorus and accordion

Salute No. 3. For tenor solo, SATB chorus, and orchestra

Requiem for the Living. For soprano, mezzo-soprano, tenor, and baritone soloists, SATB chorus, and orchestra

Les Bienfaits de la lune. For soprano and tenor soloists, SATB chorus, solo violin, string orchestra, harp, and percussion

"The Dong with the Luminous Nose." For children's chorus and instrumental ensemble

Unaccompanied Choral Works

"All and all the dry worlds lever"

"Eternal Father" (Anthem)

"Balade of Bon Counseill"

"Lenten ys come"

"Nightingales"

"Proud Music of the Storm"

"Rose kissed me Today"

"Sweet Day"

"Then Are the Woods so Empty"

"Welcome Maids of Honor"

Appendix D

Text for *Requiem for the Living*

The spelling and punctuation has been left as in the original.

1. Introduction

2. Requiem Aeternam

Breathe in us, life,
and breathing let us live,
and living breathe to wake,
and waking as a breeze of life,
alive to a lively wakefulness.
Breathe in us, life,
and living let us breathe

3. Dies Irae

a world's in travail
a world's at sea

the thunderbolt of hate
the leering fears,
the zigzag light of treason,
Typhoons of pain.

The children huddled in a moan
the haste to die
forlorness of the weak,
forgiveness of the safe.

a world's in travail
a world's at sea.

4. Confutatis

5. Tuba Mirum

the last post of the trumpet
sounds your last retreat,
and men from all the world
are on the march,
their feet,
though laden with the chain of years,
are heard,
like cymbals or a beating heart.

6. Ricordare [sic]

Tenor Solo:
Prometheus, in his chain of toil
with poverty and pain
like birds of prey,
the distant ranges of his thought unscaled,
the uncharted wave of discontent
and doubt he flounders in.

O toiling soul on earth and underground
a debtor to his debts,
a slave to his own soul.

Chorus:
Breathe in him, life,
and living let him breathe
though a world's in travail,
through a world's unrest

7. Confutatis

8. Lacrimosa

Mezzo-Soprano Solo:
Be gentle, pity, on the child asleep,
on children scared and scarred,
by horrors heaped so high
upon their tender years

Their swaddling clothes the white winding sheet
of a child.

Their cradle fear of life,
their dreams despair,
Their nurseries narrow cells,
their play
their death
old before young
sad before time.

Be gentle, pity, on the child asleep.

Chorus:
Breathe on them, life
and breathing let them live

9. Offertorium

For so shall all men live again,
and, from their living death,
Prometheus rise
and from the thunder storm of murder
the lightning choice shall flare

The cries of children,
torn and bruised and lost,
shall frame the road to child's security

and you, who coop up fears in your unrest,
take keys of hope,
and let your tears run loose,
out of the jungle of your agonies,
drag out the hyenas of the heart.

Gird up your loins for love
and reap the teeming earth.

10. Hostia [*sic*]

Soprano Solo:
O women, who bear and rear

the frightened children of our wars to be,
use now your pains,
no tear, no groan,
but pull on sheet,
but reap your fears,
that from the dark cell of your womb,
a man may leap to life.

11. Sanctus

Chorus:
Holy the work of men,
Holy their deeds,
a chain of deeds their life
and ever live their faith.
Holy!

12. Benedictus

Baritone Solo:
And let all that lives
be free from pain and sorrow
and let the future's children
inherit peace and plenty.

13. Requiem Aeternam

Chorus:
Breathe in us, life,
and breathing let us live
and living breathe to wake
and waking as a breeze of life
alive to a lively wakefulness,

Chorus and Soloists:
Breathe in us, life,
and breathing let us live.

Appendix E

Text for *Excerpta Tractati Logico-Philosophici*

The world is everything that is the case.
The world is the totality of facts.
Facts in logical space are the world.
What is the case, the fact, is the existence of atomic facts.
An atomic fact is a combination of objects.
Objects form the substance of the world.
Space, time and colour are forms of objects.
In the atomic facts objects hang one in another, like the members of a chain.
The totality of existent atomic facts is the world.
The existence and non-existence of atomic facts is the reality.
The picture is a model of reality.
The logical picture of facts is thought.
The thought is the significant proposition.
The proposition is a picture of reality.
The proposition is articulate.
The proposition shows its sense.
The proposition shows how things stand, if it is true. And it says, that they do so stand.
To understand a proposition means to know what is the case, if it is true.
The propositions show the logical form of reality.
They exhibit it.
Logic precedes every experience—that something is so.
Logic fills the world.
The world and life are one.
I am my world.

The sense of the world must lie outside the world. In the world everything is as it is and happens as it does happen.

As in death, too, the world does not change, but ceases.

Death is not an event in life.

Death is not lived through.

He lives eternally who lives in the present.

Is this eternal life not as enigmatic as our present one? The solution of the riddle of life in space and time lies outside space and time.

The solution of the problem of life is seen in the vanishing of this problem.

The riddle does not exist.

If a question can be put at all, then it can also be answered.

For doubt can only exist where there is a question; a question only where there is an answer, and this only where something can be said.

Whereof one cannot speak, thereof one must be silent.

Appendix F

The Choral Compositions of Elizabeth Maconchy in Chronological Order

1932
Two Motets for Double Chorus (12') for unaccompanied SATB chorus. Text: John Donne. Unpublished—manuscript at St. Hilda's College

1951
Six Settings of Poems by W. B. Yeats (15') for SSA chorus, clarinet, harp, and two horns optional. Unpublished—manuscript at St. Hilda's College

1962
"The Armado" (3') for SATB chorus and piano. Text: anonymous. Ricordi
Christmas Morning (17') Carol cantata, for SSA, S solo, piano; also scored for recorders, bells, cymbal, two timpani. Ricordi

1963/1964
Samson and the Gates of Gaza (35') for SATB chorus and orchestra. Chester Music

1965
Nocturnal (6') for unaccompanied SATB chorus, SAT solos. Text: Barnes, Thomas, Shelley. Chester Music

1966
"Propheta Mendax" (4') for unaccompanied SSA chorus. Text: eleventh-century Latin poems. Faber Music, Ltd.

"This Day" (2') for unaccompanied SSA chorus. Text: anonymous. Faber Music, Ltd.
"I Sing of a Maiden" (3') for unaccompanied SSAT chorus. Text: anonymous. Faber Music, Ltd.

1967
"Nowell, Nowell, Nowell" (3') for unaccompanied SAT and/or B chorus. Text: James Ryman. Cambridge Hymnal
"Twelfth Night Song" (3') for unaccompanied SA chorus with concluding round for four voices. Text: Robert Herrick. Cambridge Hymnal

1969
And Death Shall Have No Dominion (12') for SATB chorus and eight brass. Text: Dylan Thomas. Chester Music

1971
"Prayer before Birth" (5') for unaccompanied SSAA chorus. Text: Louis MacNeice. Chester Music

1973
Fly-by-Nights (20') for women's or children's voices, with harp or piano. Text: anonymous. Boosey and Hawkes

1974
"Siren's Song" (7') for soprano solo and SATB chorus. Text: William Browne. Chester Music

1975
"Christmas Night" (3') for unaccompanied SATB chorus. Text: Harleian MS ca. 1375. Chappell and Co., Ltd.
"Two Epitaphs" (3') for unaccompanied SSA chorus. Text: Francis Quarles and anonymous. Chester Music

1976
Two Settings of Poems by Gerard Manley Hopkins (8') for SATB chorus and seven brass. Chester Music

1978
Four Miniatures (8') for unaccompanied SATB chorus. Text: Eleanor Farjeon. Chester Music
The Leaden Echo and the Golden Echo (16') for SATB chorus, alto flute, viola, and harp. Text: Gerard Manley Hopkins. Chester Music
Heloise and Abelard (75') Dramatic cantata for STB soloists, SATB chorus, and orchestra. Text: Maconchy, after Heloise and Abelard. Chester Music

1979
Creatures (14') for SATB unaccompanied chorus. Text: Seraillier, Reeves, Farjeon, Rieu, Blake. Chester Music

1984

O Time Turn Back (15') for SATB chorus, wind quintet, and cello. Text: Walter Raleigh. Chester Music

1985

Still Falls the Rain (9') for unaccompanied double chorus. Text: Edith Sitwell. Chester Music

"The Bellman" (2') for unaccompanied SATB chorus. Text: Robert Herrick. Chester Music

"There Is No Rose" (3') for unaccompanied SATB chorus. Text: anonymous. Chester Music

Appendix G

Text for *Nocturnal*

I. COME
(William Barnes)

Will you come in early Spring
Come at Easter, or in May?
Or when Whitsuntide may bring
Longer light to show your way?
Will you come, if you be true,
For to quicken love anew?
Will you call in Spring or Fall?
Come now soon by sun or moon?
Will you come?

II. WILL YOU COME?
(Edward Thomas)

Will you come?
Will you come?
Will you ride
So late
At my side?
O, will you come?

Will you come?
Will you come
If the night
Has a moon,
Full and bright?
O, will you come?

Would you come?
Would you come
If the noon
Gave light,

Not the moon?
Beautiful, would you come?

Would you have come?
Would you have come?
Without scorning,
Had it been
Still morning?
Beloved, would you have come?

If you come
Haste and come.
Owls have cried;
It grows dark
To ride
Beloved, beautiful, come.

III. TO NIGHT
(Percy Bysshe Shelley)

Death will come when thou art dead,
Soon, too soon:
Sleep will come when thou art fled;
Of neither would I ask the boon
I ask of thee, beloved Night,
Swift be thine approaching flight,
Come soon, soon!

Appendix H

Text for "Siren's Song"

Steer, hither steer your winged pines,
All beaten mariners!
Here lie Love's undiscovered mines,
A prey to passengers.

The compass love shall hourly sing,
And as he goes about the ring,
We will not miss
To tell each point he nameth with a kiss:
Then come on shore,
Where no joy dies till Love hath gotten more.

William Browne

Appendix I

Text for *The Leaden Echo and the Golden Echo* (Maiden's Song from *St. Winefred's Well*)

The Leaden Echo

How to keep—is there any any, is there none such, nowhere known some, bow or brooch or
    braid or brace, lace, latch or catch or key to keep
        Back beauty, keep it, beauty, beauty, beauty, . . . from vanishing away?
        O is there frowning of these wrinkles, ranked wrinkles deep,
Down? no waving off of these most mournful messengers, still messengers, sad and stealing
    messengers of grey?
        No there's none, there's none, O no there's none,
        Nor can you long be, what you now are, called fair,
        Do what you may do, what, do what you may,
        And wisdom is early to despair:
        Be beginning; since, no, nothing can be done
        To keep at bay
        Age and age's evils, hoar hair,
Ruck and wrinkle, drooping, dying, death's worst, winding sheets, tombs and worms and
    tumbling to decay;
        So be beginning, be beginning to despair.
        O there's none; no no no there's none:
        Be beginning to despair, to despair,
        Despair, despair, despair, despair.

The Golden Echo

       Spare!
There is one, yes I have one (Hush there!);
Only not within seeing of the sun,
Not within the singeing of the strong sun,
Tall sun's tingeing, or treacherous the tainting of the earth's air,
Somewhere elsewhere there is ah well where! one,
    One. Yes I can tell such a key, I do know such a place,
Where whatever's prized and passes of us, everything that's fresh and fast flying of us,
    seems to us sweet of us and swiftly away with, done away with, undone,
        Undone, done with, soon done with, and yet dearly and dangerously sweet
        Of us, the wimpled-water-dimpled, not-by-my-morning-matched face,
        The flower of beauty, fleece of beauty, too too apt to, ah! to fleet,
        Never fleets more, fastened with the tenderest truth
To its own best being and its loveliness of youth: it is an ever-lastingness of, O it is an all
    youth!
Come then, your ways and airs and looks, locks, maiden gear, gallantry and gaiety and
    grace,
Winning ways, airs innocent, maiden manners, sweet looks, loose locks, long locks, lovelocks,
    gaygear, going gallant, girlgrace—
Resign them, sign them, seal them, send them, motion them with breath,
        And with sighs so soaring, soaring sighs deliver
        Them; beauty-in-the-ghost, deliver it, early now, long before death
Give beauty back, beauty, beauty, beauty, back to God, beauty's self and beauty's giver.
        See; not a hair is, not an eyelash, not the leastlash lost; every hair
        Is, hair of the head, numbered.
        Nay, what we had lighthanded left in surly the mere mould
Will have waked and have waxed and have walked with the wind what while we slept,
        This side, that side hurling a heavyhanded hundredfold
        What while we, while we slumbered.
O then, weary then why should we tread? O why are we so haggard at the heart, so care-
    coiled, care-killed, so fagged, so fashed, so cogged, so cumbered,
        When the thing we freely forfeit is kept with fonder a care,
        Fonder a care kept than we could have kept, kept
        Far with fonder a care (and we, we should have lost it) finer, fonder
        A care kept. Where kept? Do but tell us where kept, where.—
Yonder.—What high as that! We follow, now we follow.—Yonder, yes yonder, yonder,
    Yonder.

                        Gerard Manley Hopkins

Appendix J

The Choral Compositions of Thea Musgrave in Chronological Order

1953
Four Madrigals (8') for unaccompanied SATB chorus. Text: Sir Thomas Wyatt. Alexander Broude, Inc.

1954
Cantata for a Summer's Day (33') for SATB chorus, speaker, string quintet (including double bass), flute, and clarinet. Text: Maurice Lindsay. Unpublished but handled by Novello
"Song of the Burn" (2') for unaccompanied SATB chorus. Published separately by Novello

1961
"Make Ye Merry for Him That Is Come" (3') for unaccompanied SA and children's choir. Optional organ part available. Text: anonymous. Alexander Broude, Inc.

1962
Marko the Miser (A Tale for Children to Mime, Sing, and Play) (13') for unchanged voices, solos, narrator, recorders, clarinet, violin, guitar, glockenspiel, percussion. Text: Thea Musgrave and Frederic Samson. Chester Music
The Phoenix and the Turtle (18') for SATB chorus and full orchestra. Text: Shakespeare. Chester Music

1963
The Five Ages of Man (27') for SATB chorus and orchestra. Text: Hesiod. Chester Music

1963/1964
The Five Ages of Man (27') for SATB chorus, semichorus, orchestra, brass band. Text: Hesiod. Chester Music
"John Cook" (1') for unaccompanied SATB chorus. Text: anonymous. Novello
"Two Christmas Carols in Traditional Style" (4.5') for S solo, chorus (TB optional); oboe, clarinet, or violin solo; first violins, violas or second violins, and celli. Text: Norman Nicholson. Chester Music

1967
"Memento Creatoris" (4') for SAT soli, SATB chorus, organ *ad lib.* Text: John Donne. Chester Music

1973
Rorate Coeli (11') for unaccompanied SSATB soli, SATB chorus (eight part divisi). Text: William Dunbar. Novello

1978
"O caro m'è il sonno" (1.5') for unaccompanied STB soli, SATB chorus. Text: Michelangelo. Novello

1980
The Last Twilight (A Theatre Piece for Chorus and Instruments) (13') for SATB chorus, semichorus, twelve brass players, and percussion. Text: D. H. Lawrence. Novello

1984
"The Lord's Prayer" (4') for SATB chorus and organ. Novello

1986
The Black Tambourine (17') for unaccompanied SSA chorus, six handheld percussion instruments (finger cymbals, claves, drum, triangle, etc.). Text: Hart Crane. Novello

1987
For the Time Being (25') for unaccompanied SATB chorus and narrator. Text: W. H. Auden. Novello
Echoes Through Time (32') for SA chorus and five solo voices, five spoken roles, small chamber orchestra, and an optional set of three dancers. Text: C. E. Cooper. Novello

1992
Midnight (5') for unaccompanied SATB chorus. Text: John Keats.

1994
On the Underground. Set no. 1, On Gratitude, Love and Madness (10') for unaccompanied SATB chorus. Texts: James Berry, W. B. Yeats, Stevie Smith, Adrienne Rich, Emily Dickinson, Sheenagh Pugh. Novello
On the Underground. Set no. 2, The Strange and the Exotic (5') for unaccompanied SATB chorus. Texts: Robert Herrick, anonymous seventeenth century, Edwin Morgan. Novello

1995
On the Underground. Set no. 3, A Medieval Summer (10') for unaccompanied SATB chorus. Texts: Geoffrey Chaucer, and 13th century *Sumer is icumen in, loude sing cuckoo.* Novello

1996
Wild Winter (9') for SATB chorus and string orchestra. Texts: Wilfred Owen, Federico García Lorca, Stephen Crane, Victor Hugo, Aleksandr Sergeevich Pushkin, Francesco Petrarca, Georg Trakl.

1999
Celebration Day (18') for SATB chorus and orchestra. Text: John Dryden.

Appendix K

Text for *Rorate Coeli*

Rorate coeli desuper!

Rorate coeli desuper!
Heavens distill your balmy showers
For now is risen the bright day star
Fro' the rose Mary, flower of flowers:
The clear sun, whom no cloud devours.
Surmounting Phoebus in the East
Is coming of his heavenly towers;
Et nobis Puer natus est.

Archangels, angels, and dominations,
Thrones, potestatis, and martyrs sere,
And all ye heavenly operations,
Stars, planet, firmament, and sphere,
Fire, earth, air, and water clear,
To him give loving, most and least,
That come into so meek mannere;
Et nobis Puer natus est.

Sinners be glad, and penance do,
And thank your maker hairtfully;
For he that ye might not come to,
To you is coming full humbly,
Your souls with his blood to buy,

And loose you of the fiends arrest,
And only of his own mercy,
Pro nobis Puer natus est.

All clergy do to him incline.
And bow unto this bairn benign,
And do your observance divine
To him that is of Kingis King;
Incense his alter, read, and sing
In Holy kirk, with mind digest,
Him honouring above all thing,
Qui nobis Puer natus est.

Celestial fowls in the air
Sing with your notes upon height;
In firths and in forests fair
Be mirthful now, at all you might,
For passed is your dully night;
Aurora has the cloudis pierced,
The sun has risen with gladsome light,
Et nobis Puer natus est.

Now spring up flowers fro' the root,
Revert you upward naturally,
In honour of that blessed fruit
That raise up fro' the rose Mary;
Lay out your leaves lustily,
From dead take life now at the last
In worship of that Prince worthy,
Qui nobis Puer natus est.

Sing heaven imperial, most of height,
Regions of air make harmony;
All fish in flood and fowl of flight,
Be mirthful and make melody:
All "Gloria in excelsis" cry,
Heaven, earth, sea, man bird and beast,
He that is crowned above the sky
Pro nobis Puer natus est.

Done is a battle on the dragon black

Done is a battle on the dragon black
Our campion Christ confoundit has his force;
The gates of hell are broken with a crack,
The sign triumphal raisit is of the Cross,

The Devils trymmillis with hiddous voce,
The souls are borrowit and to the bliss can go,
Christ with his blood our ransom does endorse:
Surrexit Dominus de sepulchro.

Dungen is the deidly dragon Lucifer,
The cruel serpent with the mortal sting,
The old keen tiger, with his teeth on char,
Whilk in a wait has lain for us so long.
Thinking to grip us in his clawis strong;
The merciful Lord would not that it were so,
He made him for to fail of that fang:
Surrexit Dominus de sepulchro.

He for our sake that suffered to be slain,
And like a lamb in sacrifice was dight,
Is like a lion risen up again,
And as giant raxit him on height;
Sprungen is Aurora, radiant and bright,
On loft is gone the glorious Apollo,
The blissful day departed from the night:
Surrexit Dominus de sepulchro.

The great victor again is risen on height,
That for our quarrel to the death was wounded;
The sun that wax all pale now shines bright,
And, darkness cleared, our faith is now refounded;
The knell of mercy fro' the heaven is sounded,
The Christians are delivered of their woe,
The Jews and their error are confounded:
Surrexit Dominus de sepulchro.

The foe is chased, the battle cease,
The prison broken, the jevellouris fleit and flemit;
The war is gone, confirmed is the peace,
The fetters loosed and the dungeon temit,
The ransom made, the prisoners redeemed;
The field is won, o'ercomen is the foe,
Despoiled of the treasure that he yemit:
Surrexit Dominus de sepulchro.

William Dunbar

Appendix L

Text for *The Last Twilight*

Men in New Mexico

Mountains blanket-wrapped
Round a white hearth of desert—

While the sun goes round
And round and round the desert,
The mountains never get up and walk about.
They can't, they can't wake.

They camped and went to sleep
In the last twilight
Of Indian gods;
And they can't wake.

Indians dance and run and stamp—
No good.
White men make gold-mines and the mountains unmake them
In their sleep.

The Indians laugh in their sleep
From fear,
Like a man when he sleeps and his sleep is over, and he can't wake up.
And he lies like a log and screams and his scream is silent

Because his body can't wake up;
So he laughs from fear, pure fear, in the grip of the sleep.

A dark membrane over the will, holding a man down
Even when the mind has flickered awake;
A membrane of sleep, like a black blanket.

We walk in our sleep, in this land,
Somnambulist wide-eyed afraid.
We scream for someone to wake us
And our scream is soundless in the paralysis of sleep,
And we know it.

The Penitentes lash themselves till they run with blood
In their efforts to come awake for one moment;
To tear the membrane of this sleep . . .
No good.

The Indians thought the white man would awake them . . .
And instead, the white men scramble asleep in the mountains,
And ride on horseback asleep forever through the desert,
And shoot one another, amazed and mad with somnambulism,
Thinking death will awaken something . . .
No good.

Born with a caul,
A black membrane over the face,
And unable to tear it,
Though the mind is awake.

Mountains blanket-wrapped
Round the ash-white hearth of the desert;
And though the sun leaps like a thing unleashed in the sky
They can't get up, they are under the blanket.

                                        D. H. Lawrence

Appendix M

Text for "O caro m'è il sonno"

O caro m'è il sonno
e più l'esser di sasso
mentre che'l danno e la vergogna dura.
Non veder, non sentir
m'è gran ventura
però non mi destar,
deh, parla basso.

Oh how dear to me is sleep—
it is more the likeness of stone.
While the harm and the shame lasts,
not to see, not to hear
is for me a great fortune.
For that reason don't disturb me,
rather speak softly.

                                        Michelangelo

Bibliography

Books

Ammer, Christine. *Unsung: A History of Women in American Music*. Westport, CT: Greenwood Press, 1980.

Bowers, Jane, and Tick, Judith, eds. *Women Making Music*. Urbana: University of Illinois Press, 1987.

Bowra, C. M. *Primitive Song*. Cleveland, OH: World Publishing Co., 1962.

Boyd, Malcolm. *Grace Williams*. Composers of Wales 4. Cardiff: University of Wales Press, 1980.

Broder, Nathan, and Lang, Paul Henry, eds. *Contemporary Music in Europe: A Comprehensive Survey*. New York: G. Schirmer, 1965.

Carlson, Effie B. *Twelve Tone and Serial Composers: A Bio-Bibliographic Dictionary*. Metuchen, NJ: Scarecrow Press, 1970.

Carroll, Berenice A., ed. *Liberating Women's History: Theoretical and Critical Essays*. Urbana: University of Illinois Press, 1976.

Colles, H. C. *The Royal College of Music Jubilee Record 1833-1933*. London: Royal College of Music, 1933.

Cooper, Martin, ed. *The New Oxford History of Music: The Modern Age 1890-1960*. London: Oxford University Press, 1974.

Crighton, Ronald, ed. *The Memoirs of Ethel Smyth*. London: Viking Press, 1987.

Davey, Henry. *History of English Music*. London: J. Curwen and Sons, Ltd., 1921.

Demuth, Norman. *Musical Trends in the Twentieth Century*. London: Salisbury Square, 1952.

Dickinson, Peter, ed. *Twenty British Composers*. London: J. W. Chester, 1975.

Dieren, Bernard van. *Down Among the Dead Men*. London: Humphrey Milford, 1935.

East, Leslie. "The Problem of Communication: Two Solutions: Thea Musgrave and Gordon Crosse." In *British Music Now*, 19-31. Edited by L. Foreman. London: P. Elek, Ltd., 1975.

Elliot, Kenneth, and Rimmer, Frederick. *A History of Scottish Music*. London: BBC, 1973.

Ewen, David, ed. and comp. *Composers Since 1900: A Biographical and Critical Guide*. First Supplement. New York: H. W. Wilson and Co., 1981.

Forman, Lewis, ed. *British Choral Music: A Millennium Performing Conspectus of Nineteenth & Twentieth Century Music for Choral Societies*. Upminister: British Music Society, 2001.

Fuller, Sophie. *The Pandora Guide to Women Composers*. London: Pandora, 1994

Gray, Cecil. *A Survey of Contemporary Music*. London: Humphrey Milford, 1924.

———. *Predicaments of Music and the Future*. London: Humphrey Milford, 1936.

Halstead, Jill. *The Woman Composer: Creativity and the Gendered Politics of Musical Composition*. Aldershot, England: Ashgate, 1997.

Harries, Meirion and Susie. *A Pilgrim Soul: The Life and Works of Elisabeth Lutyens*. London: Michael Joseph, 1989.

Hartog, Howard, ed. *European Music in the Twentieth Century*. New York: Praeger, 1957.

Hixon, Donald L. *Thea Musgrave: A Bio-Bibliography*. Westport, CT: Greenwood Press, 1984.

Howes, Frank. *The English Music Renaissance*. New York: Stein and Day, 1966.

Jacobs, Arthur, ed. *Choral Music*. Baltimore: Penguin Books, 1963.

Kenyon, Nicholas. *BBC Symphony Orchestra*. London: BBC, 1981.

Lambert, Constant. *Music Ho! A Study of Music in Decline*. London: Faber and Faber, 1934.

Lepage, Jane Weiner. *Women Composers, Conductors and Musicians of the Twentieth Century: Selected Biographies*. 3 vols. Metuchen, NJ: Scarecrow Press, 1980, 1983, 1988.

Long, Kenneth R. *The Music of the English Church*. London: Hodder and Stoughton, 1971.

Lutyens, Elisabeth. *A Goldfish Bowl*. London: Cassell and Co., Ltd., 1972.

Macarthur, Sally. *Feminist Aesthetics in Music*. Westport, CT: Greenwood Press, 2002.

Mackerness, E. D. *A Social History of English Music*. London: Routledge and Kegan Paul, Ltd., 1964.

Maconchy, Elizabeth. *Ina Boyle: An Appreciation with a Select List of Her Music*. Dublin: Dolmen Press, 1974.

Mellers, Wilfrid. *Music and Society*. London: Dennis Dobson, Ltd., 1945.

————. *Studies in Contemporary Music*. London: Dennis Dobson, Ltd., 1947.

————. *Caliban Reborn: Renewal in Twentieth Century Music*. London: Victor Gollancz, Ltd., 1968.

Mitchell, Donald. *The Language of Modern Music*. London: Faber and Faber, 1963.

Neuls-Bates, Carol, ed. *Women in Music: An Anthology of Source Readings from the Middle Ages to the Present*. New York: Harper and Row, 1982.

Norris, Gerald. *A Music Gazetteer of Great Britain and Ireland*. London: David and Charles, 1981.

Opie, June. *Come and Listen to the Stars Singing: Priaulx Rainier: A Pictorial Biography*. Cornwall, Great Britain: Alison Hodge, 1988.

Pendle, Karin, ed. *Women and Music: A History*. 2nd ed. Bloomington: Indiana University Press, 2001.

Pirie, Peter J. *The English Musical Renaissance*. New York: St. Martin's Press, 1979.

Porter, Andrew. *Music of Three Seasons*. New York: Farrar, Straus, Giroux, 1978.

————. *Music of Three More Seasons, 1977-1980*. New York: Alfred A. Knopf, 1981.

Rahn, John. *Basic Atonal Theory*. New York: Longman, 1980.

Routh, Francis. *Contemporary Music*. London: English Universities Press, Ltd., 1968.

————. *Contemporary British Music: The Twenty-Five Years from 1945-1970*. London: Macdonald and Co., Ltd., 1972.

Sadie, Julie Anne, and Samuel, Rhian. *The Norton/Grove Dictionary of Women Composers*. New York: W. W. Norton & Co., 1995

Sadie, Stanley, ed. *New Grove Dictionary of Music and Musicians*. London: Macmillan Pub., Ltd., 2001.

Schafer, Murray. *British Composers in Interview*. London: Faber and Faber, 1963.

Scholes, Percy A. *The Mirror of Music, 1844-1944: A Century of Musical Life in Britain as Reflected in the Pages of Musical Times*. 2 vols. London: Oxford University Press, 1974.

Searle, Humphrey, and Robert Layton. *Britain, Scandanavia and The Netherlands*. Twentieth Century Composers, vol. 3. London: Wiedenfeld and Nicolson, 1972.

Smyth, Ethel. *The Memoirs of Ethel Smyth*. Ed. Ronald Crichton. New York: Viking Press, 1987.

Trend, Michael. *The Music Makers: Heirs and Rebels of the English Musical Renaissance from Elgar to Britten*. London: Weidenfeld and Nicolson, 1985.

Vaughan Williams, Ralph. *National Music and Other Essays*. London: Oxford University Press, 1987.

Walker, Ernest. *A History of Music in England*. London: Oxford University Press, 1952.

Wittlich, Gary. *Aspects of Twentieth-Century Music*. Englewood Cliffs, NJ: Prentice-Hall, 1975.

Wood, Henry J. *My Life of Music*. Freeport, NY: Books for Libraries Press, 1938.

Young, Percy M. *A History of British Music*. London: Ernest Benn Ltd., 1967.

Zaehner, R. C. *Mysticism Sacred and Profane*. London: Oxford University Press, 1957.

Zaimont, Judith Lang, ed. *The Musical Woman: An International Perspective*. Vol. 1. Westport, CT: Greenwood Press, 1984.

Articles

Alldis, John. "Modern Choral Music." *Composer* 33 (Autumn 1969): 8-12.

Aplvor, Denis. "Avant-garde: Then and Now." *Composer* 59 (Winter 1977): 19.

Barstow, Chris. "Anne Macnaghten." *The Strad* 94 (December 1983): 551-554.

Baxter, Timothy. "Profile: Priaulx Rainier." *Composer* 59 (Summer, Winter 1976-1977): 21-29

———. "Priaulx Rainier: A Study of Her Musical Style." *Composer* 60 (Spring 1977): 19-26.

Bender, William. "The Musgrave Ritual: Romancing the Woman Who Wasn't There." *Time*, October 10, 1977, 72.

Bennett, Richard Rodney. "Elisabeth Lutyens' Stage Works." *Tempo* 120 (March 1977): 47-48.

Blume, Mary. "Elisabeth Lutyens," *International Herald Tribune*, Saturday-Sunday, January 9-10, 1982.

Blumfeld, Harold. "Christmas Carol." *Opera Journal* 13, no. 2 (1980): 15-18.

Bowen, Meirion. "Musical Pioneer." *Guardian*, April 15, 1983.

Bradshaw, Susan. "Thea Musgrave." *Musical Times* 104 (1963): 866-868.

———. "The Music of Elisabeth Lutyens." *Musical Times* 112 (1971): 563-566.

Caruso, Michael. "Musgrave's Carol: A Modern Miracle." *Main Line Times*, December 10, 1981, 53.

Chapman, Ernest. "The Macnaghten Concerts." *Composer* 57 (Spring 1976): 13-18.

Clemens, Andrew. "Maconchy at 70." *Music and Musicians* 25 (1976-1977): 57-58.

———. "Heloise and Abelard." *Music and Musicians* 27 (1978-1979): 19.

Cole, Hugo. "Lutyens." *Guardian*, July 10, 1976.

Crutchfield, Will. "Harriet Tubman as Opera Heroine." *New York Times*, February 24, 1985, 53.

Dean, Winton. "English Music Today." *The Score* 8 (September 1953): 5-10.
————. "Mary Queen of Scots." *Musical Times* 118 (1977): 941.
Decker, Harold A. "Choral Singing in England." *Choral Journal*, May 1973, 5-7.
Driver, Paul. "Portrait of a Pioneer at 75." *The Sunday Times*, March 15, 1981, 41.
Elguera, Amalia. "The Birth of Ariadne." *The Listener* 13 (June 1974): 769.
Elias, Brian. "E. L. (1906-1983)." *Tempo* 145 (June 1983): 33.
Evans, Edwin. "Modern British Composers." *Musical Times* 60 (January 1919): 10-13.
Felton, James. "Musgrave: A Virtuoso in Debut." *The Philadelphia Evening Bulletin*, September 25, 1976, A6
————. "'Carol' Is Going to Sound Like An Opera." *The Philadelphia Evening Bulletin*, December 6, 1981, F8.
Fleming, Shirley. "Thea Musgrave's Elusive 'Ariadne.'" *New York Times*, September 25, 1977, 19.
Ford, Christopher. "Double Concerto." *Guardian* (Manchester, England), August 9, 1973.
Freedman, Guy. "Thea Musgrave: Interview." *Music Journal* 35 (1977): 4-6.
Griffiths, Paul. "Counting Your Steps." *Musical Times* 113 (1972): 683.
————. "De Amore." *Musical Times* 114 (1973): 1152.
————. "Tribute to a Pioneer." *The London Times*, July 13, 1981, 9.
Gyde, Arnold. "Britain's Young Composers Are On Parade Tonight." *The Star*, February 8, 1938.
Harris, Roger. "Heloise and Abelard." *Music and Musicians* 27 (1978-1979): 58-59.
Harrison, Max. "Lutyens, Bedford." *Musical Times* 111 (1970): 1121.
————. "70th Birthday Concert." *The Sunday Times*, November 28, 1976, 37.
Heinsheimer, Hans. "Mistress Musgrave." *Opera News* 42 (September 1977): 44-46.
Henderson, Robert. "The Phoenix and the Turtle." *Musical Times* 103 (1962): 701.
Hentoff, Nat. "Women: Their Infinite Musical Variety." *Cosmopolitan*, May 1980, 71.
Hutchings, Arthur. "Music in Britain." *The New Oxford History of Music: The Modern Age*. London: Oxford University Press, 1974.
Jennings, Paul. "Lutyens with Her Lute." *The Sunday Times*, February 18, 1973, 38.
Johnson, Tom. "Ariadne's New Voice Needs Changing." *Village Voice*, October 17, 1977, 71.
Jones, Robert. "Walking into the Fire." *Opera News* 40 (February 1976): 11-21.
Kassler, Jamie Croy. "A Goldfish Bowl." *Notes* 30, no. 3 (March 1974): 522-523.

Kay, Norman. "Thea Musgrave." *Music and Musicians* 18, no. 4 (December 1969): 34-37.

————. "Musgrave's Dance." *Music and Musicians* 18 (January 1970): 57-58.

Keener, Andrew. "E. L. Tribute Concert." *The Strad* 95 (October 1984): 389-390.

Keller, H. "The Viola as Prima Donna and Other Improbabilities." *Musical Times* 11 (1950): 321-323.

Kemp, Jeffery. "Behind the Scenes." Unpublished interview with Elisabeth Lutyens, 1974.

Kerner, Leighton. "No Humbug in Virginia, Virginia." *Village Voice*, October 17, 1977, 47.

Knight, Judyth. "Lutyens-Constantly Absorbing." *Composer* 47 (Spring 1973): 19.

Kolodin, Irving. "Second Generation Bartók." *Saturday Review*, February 7, 1976, 47.

Lea, Edward. "Notes for Women." *Musical Opinion* 96 (April 1973): 353-355.

LeFanu, Nicola. "On Being a Young Composer." *The Listener*, July 9, 1968, 56.

————. "Elizabeth Maconchy." *RCM Magazine* 83 (Autumn 1987): 113-114.

————. "Master Musician: An Impregnable Taboo?" *Contact* 31 (Autumn 1987): 4-8. See also responses by Diana Burrell ("Accepting Androgyny"), and Rhian Samuel ("Women Composers Today: A Personal View") in *Contact* 32 (Spring 1988).

Lutyens, Elisabeth. "Sermon Delivered to the Society for the Performance of New Music." *Score* 26 (January 1960): 66-67.

————. "All Our Tomorrows." Unpublished article, n.d.

————. "Essence of Our Happinesses." Unpublished article, July 2, 1971.

————. "Composers on Criticism." Unpublished article, October 1, 1971.

————. "Divide and Disrule." Unpublished article, November 1972.

Maconchy, Elizabeth. "A Short Symposium on Women Composers." *Composer* 6 (Spring 1961): 19-20.

————. "The Image of Greatness: Ralph Vaughan Williams." *Composer* 15 (Spring 1965): 10-12.

————. "Who Is Your Favorite Composer?" *Composer* 24 (Summer 1967): 20-21.

————. "A Composer Speaks." *Composer* 42 (Winter 1971-1972): 24-29.

Macnaghten, Anne. "Elizabeth Maconchy." *Musical Times* 96 (June 1955): 298-302.

————. "Anne Macnaghten." *The Strand* 94 (December 1983): 553.

————. "The Story of the Macnaghten Concerts." *Musical Times* 100 (September 1959): 460-461.

Mark, Peter. "Musgrave's 'Ariadne.'" *Opera* (London) 25 (June 1974): 476-478.

Maycock, Robert. "Inheriting the Land." *The Listener*, March 12, 1987.

Mellers, Wilfrid. "Recent Trends in British Music." *Musical Quarterly* 38 (April 1952): 185-201.

Milnes, Rodney. "Dickens into Opera." *Musical Times* 122 (1981): 818-820.

M.M.S. "Macnaghten–Lemare Concerts," *Musical Times* 76 (February 1935): 170.

Morreau, Annette. "Great Mistresses: Annette Morreau on three women taking the baton in another male-dominated world (women II)," *New Statesman,* August 25, 2003.

Morgan, Tom. "Judith Weir." *Oxford University Press Yearbook.* 1988.

Musgrave, Thea. "The Decision." *Musical Times* 108 (1967): 988-991.

———. "Starting Points." *The Listener* 81 (1969): 153.

———. "A New Viola Concerto." *Musical Times* 114 (1973): 790-791.

———. "Mary Queen of Scots." *Musical Times* 118 (1977): 625-627.

Oakes, Philip. "Lutyens Clocks In." *Sunday Times,* February 27, 1972, 34.

"Obituary: Elisabeth Lutyens." *Musical Times* 124 (May 1983): 378.

O'Loughlin, Niall. "Lutyens's 'Novenaria.'" *Tempo* 88 (Spring 1969): 55-56.

Pappenheim, Mark. "Weird World." *Radio Times,* November 26-December 2, 1988.

Payne, Anthony. "Lutyens' Solution to Serial Problems." *The Listener,* December 5, 1963, 961.

———. "Elisabeth Lutyens' Essence of Our Happinesses." *Tempo* 95 (1970): 33-34.

Porter, Andrew. "Some New British Composers." *Musical Quarterly* 51 (1969-1970): 57-58.

———. "Thea Musgrave's *Voice of Ariadne.*" *New Yorker,* October 24, 1977, 163-165.

———. "Mary." *New Yorker,* May 1, 1978, 136.

———. "Reviews." *New Yorker,* March 29, 1982, 133.

Routh, Francis, and ApIvor, Denis. "The Avant-garde: Then and Now." *Composer* 59 (Winter 1977): 19-23.

Sapp, Allen. "Thea Musgrave: A Perspective." Unpublished paper delivered Thursday, January 16, 1986, at the College-Conservatory of Music, University of Cincinnati.

Saxton, Robert. "Elisabeth Lutyens at 75." *Musical Times* 122 (1981): 368-369.

———. "Elisabeth Lutyens." *New Music 1988,* 9-21. London: Oxford University Press, 1988.

Schonberg, Harold C. "Opera Mary Queen of Scots Has US Debut in Norfolk." *New York Times,* March 31, 1978, C19.

Sharp, Geoffrey. "The Viola as Prima Donna and Other Improbabilities," *Music Review* 11 (1950): 321.

Skiba, John. "In Conversation With Elizabeth Maconchy." *Composer* 63 (Spring 1978): 7-10.

Smith, Patrick J. "Harriet, the Woman Called Moses: Thea Musgrave's New Success." *Opera* (London) 36 (May 1985): 492-493.
Smyth, Ethel. Found in a letter to the *Musical Times* 53 (April 1912): 232.
"Society of Women Musicians," news item in *Musical Times* 52 (August 1911): 535.
Specht, Richard. "Dr. Ethel Smyth." *Musical Times* 53 (March 1912): 168.
Swan, Annalyn. "Carol." *Newsweek*, December 17, 1979, 88.
Tinker, Christopher. "Imogen Holst's Music 1962-84." *Tempo* 166 (September 1988): 22-27.
Walsh, Stephen. "'Time Off' and 'The Scene Machine.'" *Musical Times* 113 (1972): 137-139.
———. "Musgrave's the Voice of 'Ariadne.'" *Musical Times* 113 (1974): 465-468.
Webster, Daniel. "A Christmas Carol: Strong in Opera Form." *The Philadelphia Inquirer*, December 7, 1978, B5.
Wells, William. "Counting Your Steps." *Notes* 29, no. 3 (March 1973): 563-54.
Williams, Grace. "Views and Revisions: The Composer Talks to A. J. Rees." *Welsh Music* 5, no. 4 (Winter 1976-1977).
———. "Grace Williams: A Self Portrait." *Welsh Music* 8, no. 5 (Spring 1987): 9-10.
Wood, Elizabeth. "Women in Music." *Signs* 6, no. 2 (1980): 283-297.
———. "Women, Music, and Ethel Smyth: A Pathway in the Politics of Music." *The Massachusetts Review* 24 (Spring 1983): 125-139.

Letters

From John Alldis to Catherine Roma, October 10, 1987.
From Christopher Bornet (Reference Librarian, Royal College of Music) to Catherine Roma, August 25, 1988.
From Ian Caddy, singer who commissioned Lutyens, to Catherine Roma, December 4, 1987.
From Susan Harries, author of forthcoming biography of Elisabeth Lutyens, to Catherine Roma, July 15, 1987, July 21, 1987.
From Nicola LeFanu to Catherine Roma, November 13, 1988, December 27, 1988.
From Thea Musgrave to Catherine Roma, January 26, 1986, October 29, 1986.
From Anthony Payne to Catherine Roma, August 8, 1988.
From Glyn Perrin, executor of Lutyens' estate, to Catherine Roma, May 16, 1986, August 5, 1986, April 7, 1988.
From Arthur Searle, assistant keeper manuscript collection, British Library, to Catherine Roma, January 28, 1987.

From Rachel Stockdale, curator manuscript collection of Elisabeth Lutyens collection, British Library, to Catherine Roma, August 8, 1988, February 20, 1987, July 29, 1987.

Interviews

With Erika Fox, March 1989
With Nicola LeFanu, February 1989
With Elizabeth Maconchy, by phone, February 1986
With Thea Musgrave, January 16, 1986
With Glyn Perrin, February 1986
With Judith Weir, March 1989
With Gillian Whitehead, February 1989

Films and Videos

"Mothers and Daughters." TV interview with Elisabeth Lutyens. Part of a series done for British television, 1981.
Elizabeth Maconchy, a film directed by Margaret Williams, 1985. Produced by the Arts Council of Great Britain.

Scores

Lutyens, Elisabeth. "The Country of the Stars." London: Novello and Co., Ltd., 1963.
————. *Excerpta Tractati Logico-Philosophici*. London: Schott and Co., Ltd., 1965.
————. *Verses of Love*. London: Novello and Co., Ltd., 1971.
————. *Counting Your Steps*. London: Olivan, 1972.
Maconchy, Elizabeth. "The Armado." London: Ricordi, 1963.
————. "Siren's Song." London: Chester Music, 1974.
————. *The Leaden Echo and the Golden Echo*. London: Chester Music, 1978.
————. *Creatures*. London: Chester Music, 1979.
————. *Nocturnal*. London: Chester Music, 1981.
Musgrave, Thea. *Four Madrigals*. London: Chester Music, 1953.
————. "John Cook." London: Novello and Co., Ltd., 1963.
————. "Memento Creatoris." London: Chester Music, 1967.
————. "Song of the Burn." London: Novello and Co., Ltd., 1974.
————. *Rorate Coeli*. London: Novello and Co., Ltd., 1977.

Bibliography

———. "O caro m'è il sonno." Novello and Co., Ltd., 1978.
———. *The Last Twilight*. Novello and Co., Ltd., 1981.
———. "The Lord's Prayer." Novello and Co., Ltd., 1984.

Index

About the Author

Catherine Roma, DMA, is associate professor of music at Wilmington College in southwestern Ohio. Her interests in the performance and study of women composers started while she was a master's student in choral conducting at the University of Wisconsin–Madison. Roma was one of the founding mothers of the women's choral movement, an international network of over seventy women's choruses, when she started Anna Crusis Women's Choir in her native Philadelphia in 1975. She began MUSE, Cincinnati's Women's Choir in 1984 after moving to Ohio to pursue graduate work at the University of Cincinnati's College-Conservatory of Music where she completed her Doctor of Musical Arts Degree in 1989. Her mentors in choral conducting and music education include Louise Christine Rebe and Dorothy Persichetti (piano teachers), Mary M. Brewer (Germantown Friends School), Elaine Brown (Singing City), Robert Fountain, Helmuth Rilling, Bernice Johnson Reagon, and Karin Pendle.

Through her association at Wilmington, Catherine founded and directs UMOJA Men's Chorus at Warren Correctional Institution in Lebanon, Ohio. She is Minister of Music at St. John's Unitarian Church in Cincinnati and is cofounder and director of the Martin Luther King Coalition Chorale. Honors include the Jane Schlissman Award for Outstanding Contributions to Women's Music (1993), Race Relations Recognition Award (1999), the GALA Legacy Award (2000), the Maurice McCracken Peace and Justice Award (2000), the Cincinnati Leading Woman Award, arts/entertainment category (2001), and the Image Maker Award, *Applause Magazine*, February 2002 in arts category.

Publications include "Women's Choral Literature: Finding Depth," in the *Choral Journal,* May 2004; "Contemporary British Composers, 1918 to the Present," in *Women and Music: A History*, ed. Karin Pendle (1991, second edition 2001); "The Healing MUSE: An interview with Kay Gardner," in *Contemporary Music Review*, Volume 16, edited by Peter Nelson and Nigel Osborne (1997); and musical transcriptions in *Continuum: The First Song Book of Sweet Honey in the Rock*, edited by Ysaye Maria Barnwell (2000).